SRA
Reading Mastery
Signature Edition

Teacher's Guide
Grade 2

Siegfried Engelmann
Susan Hanner

McGraw Hill SRA

Columbus, OH

SRAonline.com

 SRA

Send all inquiries to this address:
SRA/McGraw-Hill
4400 Easton Commons
Columbus, OH 43219

ISBN: 978-0-07-612548-7
MHID: 0-07-612548-3

3 4 5 6 7 8 9 10 BCM 13 12 11 10 09 08

The *McGraw·Hill* Companies

■■■■■■■■■■ Contents ■■■■■■■■■■

The lessons for *Reading Mastery Signature Edition,* Grade 2 provide virtually all the specific information that you need to present them. The purpose of this guide is not to repeat the specific directions that appear in the lessons, but to explain the rationale for the procedures and to provide the kind of information that you will probably need to deal with specific problems.

Introduction

Reading Mastery Signature Edition, Grade 2 is a one-year program containing 145 lessons that are designed to follow *Reading Mastery Signature Edition,* Grade 1 or *Reading Mastery Signature Edition,* Transition. All levels of *Reading Mastery Signature Edition* are research-based sequences that have been thoroughly field-tested and revised on the basis of performance of teachers and students.

Following completion of *Reading Mastery Signature Edition* Grade 2, students may go into a variety of programs. They may continue with structured reading. One such option, which is continuous with the skills and formats of Grade 2, is *Reading Mastery Signature Edition,* Grade 3.

In any case, the students who complete Grade 2 will have solid decoding skills, a relatively large reading vocabulary, and a good working knowledge of word meanings. The most important attribute students will have, however, is skill in **reading to learn.** They will be well-practiced in learning new concepts and gleaning new information from texts that they read, rather than from accompanying discussions. Their ability to "read to learn" enables them to engage in a variety of sophisticated projects involving research and reading on a variety of topics.

Many students who fail to become good functional readers have not received the kind of practice and perspectives necessary to develop proficiency in reading to learn. Their reading programs concentrated almost exclusively on stories, simple information passages, and literature.

In contrast, *Reading Mastery Signature Edition,* Grade 2 provides a very strong focus on the skills needed for students to become proficient at letting a textbook or article "teach" them something that may involve rules and evidence.

For Whom

Reading Mastery Signature Edition, Grade 2 is appropriate for students who have completed *Reading Mastery Signature Edition,* Grade 1 or *Reading Mastery Signature Edition,* Transition. It also may be used for any student who reads at about beginning second-grade level. The placement test that appears in Appendix A of this guide may be used to determine whether students meet the criteria for placement in *Reading Mastery Signature Edition,* Grade 2 or Transition.

Program Components

Teacher Support

The following teacher materials are included in *Reading Mastery Signature Edition,* Grade 2:

- **3 presentation books** provide specific teacher instructions for presenting every activity in the program.

- **An Answer Key book** contains answer keys for workbook and textbook responses.

- **The Teacher's Guide** provides a complete explanation of the program and how to teach it. Explanations of the program components indicate skills students learn. The guide provides suggestions for teaching critical exercises and for correcting more typical mistakes. The guide also discusses the mastery tests and specifies remedies for students who do not perform acceptably on these tests. The guide's Appendices include a list of spelling words, glossary, placement test, summary sheets, and reproducible blackline masters used in teaching the program. Blackline masters of family letters are also supplied to be sent home twice during the school year.

- **The Spelling Presentation Book** provides scripted material for directing the activities for 145 spelling lessons.

- **Activities across the Curriculum** provides directions and blackline masters for 39 activities that can be used throughout the program to extend and reinforce the skills that the students are acquiring.

Student Materials

The following student materials are included in *Reading Mastery Signature Edition,* Grade 2:

- **3 textbooks** with 4-color illustrations contain vocabulary lists, stories, and information passages that students read as part of every reading lesson, comprehension items for the stories and the information passages presented in the lessons, and tests 1–15.

- **Worksheets for daily lessons** provide additional comprehension activities, which are coordinated with the textbook stories.

- **Blackline masters** appearing in this guide to be reproduced for fact-game activities.

Home Connection

- **Two blackline masters** are supplied for family letters to be sent home twice a year. See Appendix K in the Teacher's Guide for English and Spanish versions.

Scheduling Lessons

The program includes daily reading lessons, daily lessons in spelling, and daily lessons for reading-related skills. The program also includes intermittent project lessons.

Daily reading lessons require 40 minutes each. They address core reading skills—decoding, comprehension, and skills in "reading to learn." The anticipated rate is that students complete one lesson per day.

Daily independent-work periods require 30 minutes each. Students need this in-school time to complete the independent work presented in the daily reading lessons.

Daily spelling lessons require 10 minutes each. They should not be scheduled in the 40 minutes allocated for the daily reading lessons. Ideally, they should occur at another time of the school day.

The time required to complete the activities in Activities across the Curriculum varies from approximately 10 minutes to about an hour. These activities should be scheduled outside of the daily reading lesson.

Each project lesson requires 40 to 80 minutes; however, some projects could require even more time. These lessons should not be scheduled as part of the daily reading period, but should occur at other times.

Also, **a daily workcheck period of 10 minutes** is highly desirable. This time could be scheduled at a time other than the reading period or could be added to the beginning of the reading period (making the reading period 50 minutes per day).

An efficient scheduling option has a daily 40-minute period in the morning for presenting the regular reading lesson and a daily 20-minute period in the afternoon devoted to spelling, and a workcheck of the students' independent work.

The chart below summarizes the time requirements for teaching *Reading Mastery Signature Edition,* Grade 2 effectively:

Time needed	Lesson type	How often
40 minutes	Reading lesson	Daily
30 minutes	Independent-work	Daily
10 minutes	Spelling	Daily
10 minutes	Workcheck	Daily
40 to 80 minutes	Project lesson	After every major story sequence
10 to 60 minutes	Activity lesson	From time to time

Lesson Types

Reading Mastery Signature Edition, Grade 2 has eight lesson types. Some are main lessons, and some are supplemental. The following chart summarizes the lesson types:

Main Lessons (1–145):	
Number	Type
118	Reading lessons (lessons 1–9, 11–14, 16–19, 21–24, etc.).
14	Reading lessons plus fluency checkouts (every 10 lessons: 15, 25, 35, etc.).
15	Test lessons (every 10 lessons: 10, 20, 30, etc. plus End-of-Program test. Test lessons include fluency checkouts.).
145	Spelling lessons (1–145, part of every reading lesson).

Supplemental Lessons (10–145):	
15	Special project lessons (following every major story sequence).
39	Activity lessons (from time to time)

For reading and spelling, the main lessons are to be presented daily. (Only the reading lessons are to be presented during the daily 40-minute reading periods. Spelling lessons and special-project lessons are to be presented during some other time of the school day.)

Reading Lessons

The teaching structures of the 145 numbered reading lessons fall into three types.

1. The first is the **regular reading lesson,** which generally consists of word attack exercises, vocabulary exercises, and one or more selections that students read during the period.

2. The second lesson type consists of a **regular reading lesson, plus a fluency checkout,** during which students individually read a 100-word passage from the preceding lesson.

3. The third type of reading lesson is the **test lesson,** which occurs every tenth lesson. The test lesson assesses the students' performance on both the content presented in the preceding nine lessons, and rate and accuracy in reading a 100-word passage. Starting with lesson 30, students also play a fact game as part of the test lesson. The facts are taken from the preceding nine lessons.

Spelling Lessons

Daily spelling lessons are presented beginning with lesson 1. These require about 10 minutes per lesson and involve no printed student material. The spelling lessons are numbered because they are to be coordinated with the reading lessons. The spelling lessons should be presented either on the same day as the corresponding reading lesson or on a later day. The spelling lessons should **not** be presented in advance of the reading lessons.

Special-Project Lessons

The 13 special-project lessons and a scavenger hunt occur intermittently, usually after students complete a major story sequence in the reading program. The special projects and the necessary materials are listed in Appendix B. The projects include making a map of a story location, completing the lyrics for a song, and acting out part of a story. The work on each project derives from rules and information that students have already mastered in the reading lessons. Some projects may require more than 80 minutes, and may take more than one day to complete. Some projects may require using computers to answer specific questions that are difficult to research through encyclopedias. (Web sites such as Ask.com are able to handle almost any question.) Some of the later projects may be started in class and then completed as homework assignments.

The special projects expand on the unique emphases of each major story sequence. The special projects: (1) provide students with information that amplifies rules or perspectives presented in main stories; (2) provide experience with cooperative learning; (3) give students an opportunity to work independently at finding information; (4) engage students in activities that reinforce self-expression.

The cycle guarantees that students learn that information applies to different contexts, that information serves as a basis for drawing inferences, and that comprehension and enjoyment of stories increases when inferences are drawn.

Activity Lessons

The lessons provide 39 activities, most of which have blackline master student material. Each activity is keyed to a specific lesson range in *Reading Mastery Signature Edition,* Grade 2. The activities cover a range of content areas, including science, social studies, and geography.

Each activity expands on the skills or information presented in the specified lessons of *Reading Mastery Signature Edition,* Grade 2. Each activity specifies the content area being explored, the materials required, and the objective.

To use the activity lessons:

- Select the activities that you wish to present and schedule them at a time when the students have completed the targeted lessons in *Reading Mastery Signature Edition* Grade 2.

- Schedule sufficient time for the activity, but don't allow so much time that activity work seriously impedes students' progress through *Reading Mastery Signature Edition* Grade 2.

- Provide students with copies of blackline masters required for most activities.

Lesson Events

The following chart shows the lesson events for each type of reading lesson. The events are listed in the order of their occurrence during the lesson. Xs indicate which events occur in lessons. Xs in parentheses indicate that the lesson event does not occur in every lesson. For example, the parentheses around the Xs for **story background** indicate that the story backgrounds do not appear in every lesson; however, when they do appear, they are presented immediately before the main-story reading.

Here is a summary of the events for **regular lessons:**

- **Oral vocabulary practice**—teacher directed. Students learn and review words and expressions that will be used in later reading selections.

- **Word-attack presentation**—teacher directed. The students read lists of words aloud and do word-meaning activities with some of the words.

- **Story Background**—teacher directed. The students orally read a short passage that presents information to be used in later reading activities. The students orally respond to specified tasks about key details of the comprehension passage.

- **Main-story reading**—teacher directed. Main stories are the primary teacher-directed activity in every regular lesson. The students orally read a long selection (between 280 and 850 words) and orally respond to specific comprehension tasks the teacher presents. Nearly all main stories have more than one part. Parts are presented on consecutive regular lessons. Some main stories (such as Eric and Tom) span more than 10 lessons. The story comprehension items refer to earlier parts as well as the part presented in the current lesson.

- **Paired practice.** This activity is part of each regular lesson and part of

Lesson Events	Regular Lesson	Fluency Checkout Lesson	Test Lesson
Oral vocabulary practice	(X)	(X)	
Word-attack presentation	X	X	
Story Background	(X)	(X)	
Main-story reading	X	X	
Paired practice	X		
Independent work	X	X	
Workcheck	X	X	
Fluency checkout		X	X
Fact game			X (starting in lesson 30)
Test of program content			X

some checkout lessons. It occurs immediately after the reading of the main story. Students work in pairs and read a specified part of that story to their partner. For paired practice, students are permanently assigned as either the A member or the B member of the pair. On alternate days, the A member reads the first part of the specified passage, and the B member reads the second part.

- **Independent work.** Students write answers to written items relating to (a) the comprehension passage, (b) the main story, (c) previously taught content, and (d) skills that students have learned (vocabulary words, deductions, sequencing, etc.). For typical lessons, some independent work appears on the student worksheet and some in the student textbook.

- **Workcheck**—teacher directed. The teacher (a) checks the students' independent work and (b) makes sure the students understand and correct the items they missed.

Fluency Checkout lessons occur every tenth lesson, starting with lesson 15. Students individually read a passage from the main story that was presented in the preceding lesson. Fluency checkout lessons are designed to give the students practice in meeting rate and accuracy criteria for oral reading.

Test lessons occur every tenth lesson, starting with lesson 10. Test lessons consist of items that test students' comprehension of the new vocabulary, information, rules, and other skills that were presented in the preceding nine lessons. Starting with lesson 20, the lessons also present a rate-and-accuracy fluency checkout on a one-hundred-word passage from the preceding lesson.

Starting with lesson 30, students also play a **fact game** in test lessons. These games provide students with practice on important facts presented in the preceding nine lessons.

Grouping the Students

If the ability level of students in the classroom is fairly homogeneous, *Reading Mastery Signature Edition,* Grade 2 may be presented to the entire class. One problem with large entire-class instruction is that the individual students do not receive as many opportunities to read aloud. For this reason, you may decide to place the most able students in one group and the lower performers in another group. All students now receive more practice with supervised reading.

The placement test that appears in Appendix A of this guide may be used to evaluate each student's entry level. Directions for administering the test and criteria for placing students in the program accompany the test.

Overview of Decoding and Comprehension Emphases

Each lesson in *Reading Mastery Signature Edition,* Grade 2 has two distinct objectives: one is decoding, the other is comprehension. The word-attack presentation deals not only with teaching decoding skills, but also with developing understanding of key words. Similarly, the story background and the main story are not simply vehicles for comprehension; important decoding objectives are also met through these activities.

The following outline summarizes the activities involved in the development of decoding rate and accuracy and the development of various comprehension skills. The outline specifies the part of the lesson or the material that develops each subskill.

I. DECODING EMPHASIS

  A. *Word-Attack Exercises*
  (presented during the first part of each lesson)

   1. *New hard words* are modeled by the teacher and then decoded by the students.

   2. *Words with similar features* (for example, all end in **S,** all have the combination **oi,** or all are compound words) are grouped together in columns and are read by the students.

   3. *Unrelated decodable words* (those that have been presented earlier or those that should be decodable by virtue of the students' skills) are grouped in columns.

  B. *Main-Story Reading Procedures*
  (presented with the main selection for each lesson)

   1. Students orally read two or three sentences for each turn.

   2. Corrections for decoding errors are provided immediately. The teacher identifies the missed word, and the student rereads the sentence in which the word appears.

   3. Students read the last part of the selection silently (starting in lesson 92).

  Note: Procedures 1 and 2 also apply to the comprehension passage.

C. *Paired Practice*

Permanently assigned pairs of students orally reread the main story to each other. Partners are to correct each other's decoding errors.

D. *Fifth-Lesson Fluency Checkouts*

Students individually read a one-hundred-word passage selected from the main story of the preceding lesson and meet a specified rate-accuracy criterion.

II. COMPREHENSION EMPHASIS

A. *Vocabulary Model Sentences*

Selected vocabulary words appear in sentences like "She survived until she was rescued."

1. Students learn what each sentence means and practice saying the sentence.

2. Students respond to tasks about the meaning of specific words.

B. *Word-Attack*

Critical vocabulary items (idioms, phrases, and individual words that will appear in stories or comprehension passages) are pretaught. The teacher tells the meaning of each vocabulary word or models how to use it.

C. *Story Background Reading*

(These passages preteach information that will appear in main stories.)

1. As the students read each passage aloud, the teacher presents specified comprehension tasks.

2. The students respond orally.

D. *Main-Story Reading Activities*

1. As the students read the story, the teacher presents specified comprehension tasks. The students respond orally.

2. The teacher presents a variety of tasks requiring recall of information, application of rules, inferences based on specific facts, and inferences based on information about different characters.

E. *Independent-Work Applications*

The students independently write answers to items that appear on the worksheets and in the textbook.

1. Some items relate to the main story that the group read.

2. If the lesson contains a comprehension passage, some items relate to the information presented in that passage.

3. Some items relate to skills (such as sequencing story events, vocabulary meanings, applying rules, alphabetizing).

4. Review items present information from earlier main stories or comprehension passages.

F. *Daily Workcheck*

   1. Independent work is checked.

   2. Students receive same-day feedback on their independent work performance. (They receive information on the correct answers to all items.)

G. *Tenth-Lesson Fact Games*
(starting in lesson 30)

   1. The students play a game in which they orally respond to comprehension items.

   2. These comprehension items cover key concepts and facts from earlier lessons. The items are particularly important because they will recur in later lessons.

H. *Tenth-Lesson Tests*
Students write answers to items that deal with rules, vocabulary meanings, and information presented in the preceding nine lessons.

The Decoding Emphasis

The decoding emphasis involves a cycle that introduces new decoding words and word families, presents these words in different story contexts, and provides practice in meeting oral reading rate-accuracy criteria. Both the decoding vocabulary and the various decoding-practice activities are coordinated in word-attack presentations, in group story readings, and, finally, in fluency checkouts.

Students read selections that are composed entirely of words or decodable elements taught earlier in *Reading Mastery Signature Edition,* Grade 2.

The Cycle for Developing Decoding Skills

The cycle for introducing a decoding word in *Reading Mastery Signature Edition,* Grade 2 begins with the word appearing in the word-attack lists of two or three lessons. Then the word appears in reading selections. This development of decoding words ensures that students receive practice in reading words in sentence contexts after these words have been presented in lists.

Word-Attack Presentation

The first decoding activity in every lesson is the word-attack presentation, during which the students read ten to thirty words aloud.

- For words that appeared earlier or that are decodable the teacher asks, What word?

- Words that would probably be difficult to read are first modeled by the teacher, then read by the students. Some words are also spelled. For example: Word 1 is **actually.** What word? *Actually.* Spell **actually.** *A-C-T-U-A-L-L-Y.*

- To show students structural or phonemic similarities of different word families, the teacher presents groups of words that have common features. On page 16 are the word-attack words from lesson 52. Note that the words in columns 2 and 4 have endings, and the words in column 3 are compound words.

1
1. giant
2. special
3. enormous
4. announcement
5. disappeared

2
1. frisky
2. blocks
3. bothered
4. freezing
5. checked
6. sparkling

3
1. grandchildren
2. sidewalks
3. bulkhead
4. whirlpool

4
1. swirled
2. tanks
3. smelly
4. weighs
5. billows

5
1. bow
2. stern
3. frost
4. grew
5. November

6
1. early
2. fuel
3. thirsty
4. thirstier

- For each word whose meaning may not be familiar to the students, the teacher gives an explanation of the meaning. Below is the teacher presentation script for column 5 of the word-attack exercise.

Column 5

y. Find column 5. ✔
- (Teacher reference:)

1. bow	**4. grew**
2. stern	**5. November**
3. frost	

z. Word 1 rhymes with **how.** What word? (Signal.) *Bow.*
a. Word 2. What word? (Signal.) *Stern.*
- The bow is the front of a ship. The stern is the back of the ship. What do we call the front of a ship? (Signal.) *Bow.*
- What do we call the back of a ship? (Signal.) *Stern.*
b. Word 3. What word? (Signal.) *Frost.*
- Frost is frozen water that forms on grass during cold nights. When the temperature goes up in the morning, the frost disappears.

c. Word 4. What word? (Signal.) *Grew.*
- Word 5. What word? (Signal.) *November.*
d. Let's read those words again.
- Word 1. What word? (Signal.) *Bow.*
- (Repeat for words 2–5.)
e. (Repeat step d until firm.)

Main-Story Decoding

Following the word-attack part of the lesson, the group reads the story background and all or part of the main story aloud. As students progress through the program, less of the main story is read aloud. At first, they read only about 50 words silently. Later, they read 100 words or more.

The teacher calls on individual students to take turns, each reading two or three sentences. Every main story has an **error limit** based on two errors per hundred words in the story. If the group exceeds the error limit, the students are to reread the main story until they read within the specified error limit.

The main stories contain recently introduced words. The stories, therefore, provide word-recognition practice with these words. The error limit for the story helps the students develop effective strategies for learning new words: (1) The students quickly learn that words appearing in the word-attack lists will appear in main stories, (2) They learn that if they are to read the stories within the error limits, they should pay attention to these words when they appear in the lists.

Paired-Reading Practice

The purpose of paired reading is to provide students with an opportunity to read a relatively long passage without interruption. Although students receive oral reading practice during the main-story reading, they usually read only two or three sentences at a time, and their reading may be interrupted with comprehension items. The paired-reading practice takes only 5 to 8 minutes for each lesson and makes a marked difference in the fluency performance of students.

Fluency: Rate/Accuracy

Every fifth lesson includes a fluency checkout, beginning with lesson 15. Students individually read a one-hundred word passage to a checker. The purpose of the fluency checkout is to ensure that students are progressing acceptably in oral decoding rate and accuracy. The passage that they read for the fluency checkout is taken from the preceding lesson. To pass the fluency checkout, the student reads the passage in less than a minute and makes no more than two errors.

The Comprehension Emphasis

Reading Mastery Signature Edition, Grade 2 has a comprehension emphasis on the facts, rules, and perspectives that are presented in what the students read. The program also has a vocabulary-building emphasis.

Vocabulary Emphasis

Model sentences are the principal vehicle for expanding students' vocabulary and for introducing words that will be in upcoming selections. In addition to the model sentences, the teacher presents vocabulary information for some words as part of the word-attack exercises.

Model Vocabulary Sentences

The first model sentence is introduced in lesson 4. Others follow about every three lessons. A list of sentences appears in the back of the student textbooks (and Appendix C of this guide). Students refer to this list when learning new sentences.

Each model sentence goes through an eight-step cycle.

1. The sentence is introduced. Students read the sentence. The teacher explains the key words (two or three new words that are in the sentence). Then students answer questions about the key words. For example, for the sentence **They waded into the stream to remove tadpoles** the teacher asks these questions:

   What word tells that they got rid of something?

   What word tells that they walked through water that was not very deep?

   What's the name of baby frogs or toads?

2. Later in the same lesson in which the model sentence is introduced, students review what they have learned about the model sentence.

3. In the following lesson, students review the model sentence.

4. In the third lesson of the cycle, students review the last three model sentences that had been introduced.

5. Later in that lesson, students do written tasks in which they write answers to questions about the key words.

6. In the next lesson, students work with the two most recent sentences, which are presented with key words missing. Students write the complete sentences. (For example, the model sentence would appear as: They ▆▆▆ into the stream to ▆▆▆ ▆▆▆.)

7. A verbal exercise appears periodically. The teacher says part of the sentence but stops just before a key word. Students say the next word.

8. The test in every tenth lesson contains skill items that assess the students' knowledge of vocabulary words presented in the model sentences that were introduced and sufficiently reviewed during the preceding nine lessons.

Vocabulary During Word Attack

The teacher script provides "definitions" for those words that students may not know. These descriptions often show the students how to use the word. There is no attempt to provide students with **a variety of meanings of the word,** but merely to illustrate the meaning that will be used in the upcoming selection.

Here are some examples:

Impression. When you have an **impression** about something, you have an idea about that thing. If you have the **impression** that somebody is watching you, you have the idea that somebody is watching you. What's another way of saying, **She had the idea that she was working slowly?** *She had the impression that she was working slowly.*

Motion. Here's how you **motion** to come over here. (Motion.) Show me how you **motion** for somebody to move back.

Respond. When you **respond** to someone, you **answer** them. Here's another way of saying **He answered the question: He responded to the question.** What's another way of saying **He answered the question?** *He responded to the question.*

When some of these vocabulary words appear in subsequent word-attack presentations, the teacher presents tasks that require students to use the word correctly.

Definitions for all vocabulary words appear in Appendix D of this guide and at the end of textbook C.

Developing Comprehension of Facts, Rules, and Perspectives

As decoding skills are being developed through the various lesson activities, comprehension skills are also being developed for interpreting and using facts, rules, and information about unique story-character perspectives. The general skills students learn include cause and effect, literal meaning, inferential meaning, main idea, and sequencing of events. The program presents content and practice for these skills.

Here is a summary of the sequence for developing these skills:

1. Information is introduced in a comprehension passage.

2. Within two lessons of the introduction, the information is used in the main story.

3. A variation of the information also appears in the independent-work items.

4. The items are reviewed in subsequent lessons.

5. Information that is particularly important or difficult appears in the fact games or in fact reviews. The game format provides the students with massed practice on a lot of information.

6. The tenth-lesson tests assess students' understanding of the information.

7. The final step is the integration of recent information with information taught earlier. This integration provides for increasingly complex applications and review. For major story sequences, the integration culminates with a special project, in which students research additional facets of the story theme.

General Comprehension Skills

The comprehension skills that are traditionally presented in developmental reading series stress general skills such as literal comprehension, main idea, fact versus opinion, context clues, and sequencing of events. *Reading Mastery Signature Edition,* Grade 2 is organized so that these skills are taught in a cumulative manner, which means that a particular skill is practiced not merely as a part of a few lessons, but is practiced repeatedly as part of many lessons. This cumulative practice ensures that the students work with the various skills in a variety of story and information contexts.

The table on page 20 summarizes the comprehension skills emphasized in each of the larger story series in *Reading Mastery Signature Edition,* Grade 2. (Each story series listed spans at least three lessons.) The lesson numbers for each series are indicated in the table. If the series strongly emphasizes a particular skill, the skill is marked with an asterisk (*). If the emphasis is not as strong, it is marked with a checkmark (✔).

As the table shows, literal comprehension, cause and effect, supporting evidence, and information recall activities are part of each story series. In addition to providing practice in these four categories of comprehension skills, each story series has at least one unique focus. For example, the series about Herman the Fly (a fly who gets on a jet plane and travels around the world) presents strong comprehension emphasis on sequencing, context clues, viewpoint, supporting evidence, interpretation of feelings, map skills, reality versus fantasy, and information recall.

Table of Cumulative Comprehension Emphasis

* = strong emphasis
✔ = not as strong

	4–6 (Little Apple Tree)	15–23 (Goad)	25–35 (Nancy)	37–52 (Herman)	54–63 (Linda & Kathy)	65–67 (Trojan Horse)	68–78 (Bertha)	86–88 (Horses)	89–106 (Andrew Dexter)	108–111 (Word Bank)	113–122 (Toby)	123–127 (Word Bank)	129–145 (Eric & Tom)
Literal comprehension	✔	✔	✔	✔	✔	✔	✔	✔	✔	✔	✔	✔	✔
Main idea	✔	*	*	✔	*	✔	✔		*	✔	✔	✔	✔
Sequencing	*	✔	✔	*	✔	✔		*	✔		*	✔	*
Cause and effect	*	*	✔	✔	✔	*	✔	✔	✔	*	✔	*	✔
Fact vs. opinion		✔				*	✔		✔	✔	*	✔	✔
Context clues		✔	*	*	✔		*		*	*	*	*	✔
Viewpoint	*	✔	*	*	✔	*	✔		*	*	*	*	*
Supporting evidence (relevant details)	*	✔	*	*	✔	✔	*	*	*	*	*	*	✔
Character development (Interpreting feelings, inferring motives, predicting behavior)	*	✔	*	*	*	✔			*	✔	*	✔	*
Map skills		*		*		✔	✔				*		*
Reality vs. fantasy	✔	*	*	*		*			*	*	✔	*	*
Information recall	✔	*	*	*	*	*	*	*	*	*	*	*	*
Reference-book skills		✔									✔		

Facts, Rules, and Perspectives

The grouping of comprehension skills according to broad traditional categories (such as supporting evidence) does not suggest the specific facts, rules, and perspectives that are introduced. Following is a summary of the facts, rules, and perspectives that are developed in *Reading Mastery Signature Edition,* Grade 2. The perspectives are developed through learning the rules and facts.

The major **rules** developed in *Reading Mastery Signature Edition,* Grade 2 are:

- **Measurement rules** (based on facts about centimeters, meters, miles, grams, miles per hour, seconds, degrees, inches, yards, minutes).

- **Location rules** (based on facts about the United States, Canada, Mexico, Japan, Egypt, Greece, Italy, Turkey, China, the Pacific Ocean, New York City, San Francisco, Salt Lake City, Denver, Chicago, California, Alaska, Australia).

- **History rules** (based on facts about the Trojan war, cave people, the San Francisco earthquake of 1906, future time, the Revolutionary War, Columbus discovering America, the Viking age, and ancient Greece and Egypt).

- **Classification rules** (based on facts about insects, spiders, toads and frogs, trees, types of vehicles, warmblooded and cold-blooded animals, camels, horses, dinosaurs, kangaroos, peacocks, pigs).

- **Science rules** (based on facts about water characteristics, winds, temperature, and weather changes).

The major **perspectives** presented in *Reading Mastery Signature Edition,* Grade 2 are:

- **Physical geography perspective** (earthquakes, land masses, oceans).

- **Behavior and feeling perspectives** (comparison of human and non-human responses to the same situation, projections of how the reader would behave in various situations, predictions about how a character will behave in a new situation based on information about the character's tendencies).

- **Temporal perspective** (comparison of how things were done during different historical time periods—what people thought was handsome dress in 1900, how Vikings ate, comparison of how modern people and the ancient Egyptians would move grain and other goods).

- **Size perspective** (comparison of objects viewed by average-sized beings and by very small beings—how a drop of water looks to them, how it feels to fall from a high place, how much they have to eat with respect to their body weight).

- **Distance perspective** (comparison of different trips—for instance, the distance from New York to San Francisco compared with the distance from San Francisco to Japan).

- **Place perspective** (comparison of building materials, customs, language, means of conveyance, dress of people from different places).

Preparing to Teach

This section of the guide provides you with specific, technical information about what you will be teaching and some of the problems students may have with the presentations. The purpose is to provide you with the information and the general cautions you need to **guarantee** that the students move through the program smoothly.

The guide is a tool that you should refer to throughout the year as part of your preparation for teaching the program.

1. Don't begin the program until you have studied this section of the guide.

2. Practice presenting the various exercises before you present the first lessons to the students. Don't simply read them over and assume that you will be able to present them well. Read the script aloud. Present the signals the students are to respond to. Practice saying the corrections. Make sure you can smoothly present any new exercise type that is scheduled for upcoming lessons. During the first part of the program, a fair amount of practice may be required. For later lessons, less preparation is needed.

General Teaching Strategies

When teaching *Reading Mastery Signature Edition,* Grade 2 you will be engaged in various types of activities.

- You will present model sentences and word-attack exercises.

- You will direct the students in the group reading of comprehension passages and main stories. (As they read, you will present specified oral comprehension tasks.)

- You will monitor students as they do their independent work.

- You will provide a daily workcheck and record the number of errors students make on their independent work.

- For lessons that involve individual fluency checkouts and fact games, you will monitor the fluency checkouts and games.

- You will provide remedies for students who do not pass tenth-lesson tests.

Here is a summary of the general techniques that you will use.

Get into the lesson quickly. No discussions are necessary.

Teach to mastery. Use the following guidelines:

- Repeat tasks if students are not firm.

- Use clear signals. All signals have the same purpose: They trigger a simultaneous response from the group. All signals have the same rationale: If you get the group to respond simultaneously (with no student leading the others) you will receive good information about the performance of the students. At the same time, students will receive more frequent practice than they would using individual responses.

- Reinforce good performance. Make your praise specific. If the students have just completed a difficult word list with no errors tell them what they did: You read without any mistakes. Good for you. Praise students for following the rules you present.

Pace the exercises. Since a great deal of information must be taught during the daily presentation, it is important for you to move quickly, but not to rush the students so much that they make mistakes. To ensure a smoothly paced lesson, you should become familiar with the exercises before presenting them. You must be able to present them without having to refer to the page for every word. Fast pacing is important for the following reasons:

- It reduces the problems of managing students and maintaining on-task behavior. Studies have shown that faster pacing secures more student interest and reduces management problems.

- Fast pacing results in greater student achievement. With faster pacing, a teacher can cover more material in a fixed amount of time and provide more student practice in that time.

- Many tasks become more difficult when they are presented slowly. Slower pacing places greater memory demands on students. Faster pacing, on the other hand, reduces memory load.

Monitor independent work. Intermittently monitor students as they do their independent work. Make sure that students are working at a reasonable rate, but are not looking up answers to items and are not copying.

Using the Teacher-Presentation Scripts

The script for each lesson indicates how to present the structured activities. The lesson is a script that shows what you say, what you do, and what the students' responses are to be.

What you say appears in blue type:

> You say this.

What you do appears in parentheses:

> (You do this.)

The responses of the students are in italics:

> *Students say this.*

> *[Individual student says this.]*

Follow the specified wording in the script. While wording variations from the script are not always dangerous, you will be assured of communicating clearly with the students if you follow the script exactly. The wording in the teacher presentation books is succinctly controlled. The tasks are arranged so they focus on important aspects of what the students are to do. Although you may initially feel uncomfortable "reading" from a script, follow the scripts very closely; try to present them as if you're saying something important to the students. If you do, you'll soon find that working from a script is not difficult and that students indeed respond well to what you say.

Conventions

Samples of the teacher presentation script appear on page 26.

The arrows show the six different things you'll do that are not spelled out in the script. You'll signal to make sure that group responses involve all the students. You'll "firm" critical parts of the exercises. For some exercises, you'll write things on the board.

Arrow 1: Signals for Group Responses

(Signal.) and (Tap.)

Some tasks call for group responses. If students respond together with brisk, unison responses, you receive good information about whether the students are performing correctly. The simplest way to direct students to respond together is to signal or tap in a predictable cadence — just like the cadence in a musical piece. By listening carefully to the responses, you can tell both which students make mistakes and which ones respond late, copying those who responded first. As a result, you are able to correct specific mistakes, maximize the amount of practice, and evaluate the performance of each student.

Arrows labeled 1 on page 26 specify (Signal.) for the student responses **be, become,** and **taps** for the student spelling of **become** (a series of responses).

Using Signals

To signal the group to respond:

1. Say the task specified in the presentation script.

2. Pause.

3. Clap, or make another auditory signal such as a tap or a finger snap. (An auditory signal is necessary because the students are not looking at you but at the material they are reading.)

Here are procedures for effective signaling:

- Don't signal while talking. Talk first, then signal.

- Always maintain a time interval of about one second between the last word of the instructions or question and the signal. Signal timing should be consistent so students can respond together.

- Require students to respond together, on signal.

Column 3

k. Find column 3. ✔ ← ③

⑤ → • (Teacher reference:)

1. <u>be</u>come	4. <u>sound</u>ly
2. <u>sob</u>bing	5. <u>dar</u>ling
3. <u>your</u>self	6. <u>in</u>stead

• These words have more than one syllable. The first syllable is underlined.

l. Word 1. What's the first syllable? (Signal.) *be.*

• What's the whole word? (Signal.) ← ① *Become.*

• Spell **become.** Get ready. (Tap for each letter.) *B-E-C-O-M-E.*

m. Word 2. What's the first syllable? (Signal.) *sob.*

• What's the whole word? (Signal.) *Sobbing.*

n. Word 3. What's the first syllable? (Signal.) *your.*

• What's the whole word? (Signal.) *Yourself.*

o. Word 4. What's the first syllable? (Signal.) *sound.*

• What's the whole word? (Signal.) *Soundly.*

p. Word 5. What's the first syllable? (Signal.) *dar.*

• What's the whole word? (Signal.) *Darling.*

q. Word 6. What's the first syllable? (Signal.) *in.*

• What's the whole word? (Signal.) *Instead.*

r. Let's read those words again, the fast way.

• Word 1. What word? (Signal.) *Become.*

• (Repeat for words 2–6.) ← ⑤

s. (Repeat step r until firm.) ← ②

Column 4

t. Find column 4. ✔

• (Teacher reference:)

1. couple	4. important
2. whirl	5. expression
3. moments	6. swirl

u. Word 1. What word? (Signal.) *Couple.*

• (Repeat for words 2–6.)

v. (Repeat step u until firm.) ← ②

Individual Turns ← ⑥

(For columns 1–4: Call on individual students, each to read one to three words per turn.)

EXERCISE 1

Vocabulary Review

a. You learned a sentence about how you measure your weight.

• Everybody, say that sentence. Get ready. (Signal.) *You measure your weight in pounds.*

• (Repeat until firm.) ← ②

- To correct mistakes of not following the signal, show students exactly what you want them to do:

  I'm good at answering the right way.

  My turn: Spell **become.** Get ready.

  (Tap) **B**...(tap) **E**...(tap) **C**...(tap) **O**...(tap) **M**...(tap) **E**.

  Let's see who can do it just that way:

  Your turn. Spell **become.** Get ready. (Tap for each letter.) *B-E-C-O-M-E.*

- **Do not respond with the students** unless you are trying to work with them on a difficult response. You present only what is in blue. You do not say the answers with the students, and you should not move your lips or give other nonverbal clues about what the answer is.

Signals are very important early in the program. After students have learned the routine, the signals are not as critical because the students will be able to respond on cue with no signal. That will happen, however, only if you consistently present signals with the same predictable timing.

Arrow 2: Firming

→

(Repeat until firm.)

Wherever there's a signal, there's a place where students may make mistakes. You correct mistakes as soon as you hear them. A correction may occur during any part of the teacher presentation that calls for students to respond. It may also occur in connection with what students are writing.

- Mistakes on oral responses include saying the wrong thing or not responding. To correct: **You say the correct answer; then repeat the task the students missed.** For example:

  You learned a sentence about how you measure your weight. Everybody, say that sentence. Get ready. (Signal.)

If some students do not respond, respond slowly, or say an incorrect sentence, a mistake has occurred. As soon as you hear a mistake, you **say the correct answer:**

  Here's the sentence about how you measure your weight: You measure your weight in pounds.

Repeat the task:

  Everybody, say that sentence. Get ready. (Signal.)

A special correction is needed when correcting mistakes on tasks that teach a series of things. This type of correction is marked with the notation:

(Repeat step _ until firm.)

An example of this kind of task appears on the next page. The bracket shows a section of the presentation that is to be repeated following a mistake:

Fact Review

a. Let's review some facts you have learned. First we'll go over the facts together. Then I'll call on each of you to do some facts.

b. Everybody, tell me how long ago eohippus lived. Get ready. (Signal.) *38 million years ago.* (RF/R)

• Tell me when the story of Troy took place. Get ready. (Signal.) *3,000 years ago.* (RF/R)

• Electricity can turn any steel bar into a magnet. Tell me what those magnets are called. Get ready. (Signal.) *Electromagnets.* (RF/R)

• Tell me what country we live in. Get ready. (Signal. Accept appropriate response.) (APK)

• (Repeat step b until firm.) ← **2**

When you "repeat until firm," you follow these steps:

1. **Correct the mistake.** (Tell the answer and repeat the task that was missed.)

2. **Return to the beginning of the bracketed part and present the entire part.** For example, students miss the third task (Tell me how long a football field is.).

   You tell the answer: 100 yards.

   You repeat the task: Tell me how long a football field is.

   You return to the first task in the bracketed part and repeat the entire part: Let's go back. Tell me which comes first in a storm, lightning or thunder . . . etc.

Arrow 3: Monitoring Students

→

(**Observe students** and **give feedback.**) and ✔

SENTENCE COPYING

a. (Write on the board:)

Toads love to eat flies.

b. You're going to write this sentence.

• (Call on a student to read the sentence.)

c. Everybody, turn your paper over. ✔ ← **3**

• Write the sentence on the top line. (Observe students and give feedback.) ← **3**

d. Later you can write the sentence two more times on the lines below. **3**

The arrows labeled 3 show a checkmark (✔) or the direction (**Observe students and give feedback.**). These script conventions indicate how you are to monitor student performance.

The ✔ is a note to see whether the students have touched the part of the page you refer to. If you tell them to **turn their paper over,** or **touch column 2,** you check to see that they are doing that. Your check requires only a second or two. Monitor the responses of several "average performing" students. If their responses are acceptable, proceed with the presentation.

The (**Observe students and give feedback.**) direction implies a more elaborate response on your part. You sample more students and you give feedback, not only to individual students, but also to the group. Here are the basic rules for what to do and what not to do when you observe and give feedback:

• Circulate to make sure that you can see all of the students' papers.

- **As soon as students start to work, start observing.** As you observe, make comments to the whole class. Focus these comments on students who are following directions, working quickly, and working accurately. Wow, a couple of students are almost finished. I haven't seen one mistake so far.

- When students raise their hands to indicate that they are finished, acknowledge them.

- **If you observe mistakes, do not provide a great deal of individual help.** For example, if the directions tell students to circle the answer and some students underline it, tell them, You didn't follow the directions for number 4. Read the directions and do what they say.

If there are serious problems with part of the independent work, repeat it during the next reading period. Do not proceed in the program if the students are making a high rate of errors.

Arrow 4: Board Work

→

What you write on the board is indicated in blue display boxes. In the sample exercise on page 28, you write the sentence **Toads love to eat flies.**

Arrow 5: Script Conventions

→

(Repeat for words 2–6.) and (Teacher reference:)

Sometimes teachers lose their place in the teacher presentation script. Teachers also have difficulty keeping track of where the students are supposed to be touching in their textbooks or workbooks. Arrow 5 on page 26 shows two script conventions that enable you to more easily track what you and the students are supposed to be doing.

Step r instructs teachers "Repeat for words 2–6." Teachers are to repeat: Word ___. What word? (Signal.) Repeat for the remaining words **sobbing, yourself, soundly, darling, instead.** You don't have to read the script for those words. So you are able to attend more to what the students are doing. Here is what you would say:

r. Let's read those words again, the fast way.
- Word 1. What word? (Signal.) *Become.*
- Word 2. What word? (Signal.) *Sobbing.*
- Word 3. What word? (Signal.) *Yourself.*
- Word 4. What word? (Signal.) *Soundly.*
- Word 5. What word? (Signal.) *Darling.*
- Word 6. What word? (Signal.) *Instead.*

The presentation script provides a teacher reference that shows the students' material.
- (Teacher reference:)

1.	become	4.	soundly
2.	sobbing	5.	darling
3.	yourself	6.	instead

Refer to the teacher references as you monitor students' responses to this activity.

By looking at the teacher reference you don't have to peek at a student's textbook to see what the next word is. Using teacher references can help free you from the script without straying from the wording the script specifies. For most word lists, you'll use the same wording for all words. Once you know the wording (specified for the first word in the list) you can use the teacher reference to follow the same format shown for the first word to direct the other words.

Arrow 6: Individual Turns

Individual turns occur routinely as part of a word-attack presentation that has more than one column of words. Several other structured exercise types, such as fact reviews, also call for individual turns.

Think of individual turns as a diagnostic tool that lets you know if the students are firm on the material you just presented to the group. The general procedure for presenting individual turns is to present them only when you think the students are firm on the group tasks.

Call on a sufficient number of individual students to let you know whether they have mastered the content. You should not try to give every student a turn on every task, but rather you should sample the group in a way that does not consume a lot of time. If there are 25 students in the group, you might present tasks to 7 students. Of these 7, sample 4 students who may be weak on the material and 3 others. If students in this sample are firm, the others in the group are probably also firm.

Teaching to the Group

If the group has problems, you'll correct their mistakes or firm students on the content that has not been mastered. If the group is firm, you'll speed up the presentation and move on.

To adjust the presentation to the performance of the group, you have to attend to individuals within the group. Although all the students are supposed to have the skills needed to perform well in *Reading Mastery Signature Edition* Grade 2, there will be a range of individual variation.

This range in ability raises a question about whether you should adjust your presentation to the higher performers in the group, those in the middle, or the lower performers. Here are the guidelines:

- **If some students should not really be in the group** (according to their placement-test performance or performance on the lessons), **do not teach to them.** Either place them in a group that is appropriate for their performance level, or try to find a way to give them additional practice outside of the scheduled reading period. (One plan that may work is to have them read to a higher-performing student on a daily basis.)

- **If all students are appropriately placed, teach to the students who tend to be lower but who tend not to be the slowest in the group.** If you teach to the slowest, you may make the presentation tedious for most of the other students, and you will not move through the lessons as quickly as you should. If you teach to the higher performers, you will make it difficult for possibly half of the students. However, if you gauge your presentation to the performance of the lower students, you will provide a little more practice than the higher students require, but the presentation will not be significantly slowed for them. The presentation will also be careful enough that the lowest students in the group will benefit from it about 80 percent of the time. At that level, they will master the material (even if they need some additional practice).

- **Provide students with very unambiguous models of what you expect them to do.** Do not praise them for sloppy approximations, but also do not lose patience with them. Repeat material until they can perform perfectly. Unless you provide such a model, you're asking students to improve when they are not exactly sure what constitutes improvement.

- **Expect students to accelerate.** If you place students appropriately, initially teach them to a very hard criterion of performance, and show them what you expect them to do, they will learn faster and faster. Furthermore, they will enjoy learning much more.

Teaching the Lessons

This section gives information about teaching each part of the lesson.

Vocabulary Exercises

General Information

These exercises are the first in the lesson. They focus on model sentences and the meaning of several key words. The activities are oral. The expectation is that the students will perform very well on the exercises. Students should not require much time to respond, and their responses should be correct.

The exercise below is from lesson 37. The exercise introduces the vocabulary sentence: **Several paths continued for a great distance.** The key words are **several, continued, distance.** The focus is on the specific meaning used in the vocabulary sentence.

EXERCISE 1

Vocabulary

a. **Find page 338 in your textbook.** ✔
- Touch sentence 9. ✔
- This is a new vocabulary sentence. It says: Several paths continued for a great distance. Everybody, read that sentence. Get ready. (Signal.) *Several paths continued for a great distance*.
- Close your eyes and say the sentence. Get ready. (Signal.) *Several paths continued for a great distance*.
- (Repeat until firm.)

b. The sentence says that **several** paths continued. That's more than two paths but less than many paths. Maybe there were four paths, maybe there were three or five. There were not fifty paths.

c. Several paths **continued.** If they continued, they kept on going. What's another word for **kept on going?** (Signal.) *Continued*.

d. A great distance is a very long way. The paths went for many miles. If the paths went for a **short** distance, they would not go very far. What's another way of saying **a very long way?** (Signal.) *A great distance*.

e. Listen: Several paths continued for a great distance.
- Everybody, say the sentence. Get ready. (Signal.) *Several paths continued for a great distance*.
- (Repeat until firm.)

f. What word refers to more than two but less than a lot? (Signal.) *Several*.
- What word means **kept on going?** (Signal.) *Continued*.
- What part means **a long way?** (Signal.) *A great distance*.
- (Repeat step f until firm.)

Presenting Vocabulary Exercises

Follow these guidelines when presenting the exercises.

1. Make sure that the students produce good unison responses. Don't permit droning responses when students say the sentence.

2. Make sure that students are firm in saying the sentence. In step a, you repeat the sentence until firm. For

some sentences, students may have to say it three or more times. If students are not firm in saying the sentence, however, they will have problems when the sentence is used in this lesson and reviewed in later lessons.

3. Don't make repeating the sentence seem like punishment. If you respond to these exercises as fun or challenges that you look forward to, the students will respond the same way. Keep it upbeat and fast moving: Once more. Get ready . . .

4. Make sure students are firm on what the key words mean. In step f, you present questions about the key words. If students are not perfectly firm on all the answers, they'll have problems later. So don't be afraid to repeat items that have weak responses. And don't be afraid to use individual turns for students that produce weak or questionable responses.

5. Use the vocabulary review tasks as an indicator of how well students learn the new material. The review task below is presented later in lesson 37 and serves as a delayed test on the new sentence. If students do not do well on these same-day reviews, you may need to provide more practice on the exercises that introduce the sentences. (This review task is also presented in the next lesson.)

EXERCISE 3

Vocabulary Review

a. Here's the new vocabulary sentence: Several paths continued for a great distance.
 • Everybody, say the sentence. Get ready. (Signal.) *Several paths continued for a great distance.*
 • (Repeat until firm.)

b. What word means **kept on going?** (Signal.) *Continued.*
 • What word refers to more than two but less than a lot? (Signal.) *Several.*
 • What part means **a long way?** (Signal.) *A great distance.*

6. Expect student performance to improve **if you bring them to mastery in the early lessons.** You'll find that they tend to learn new sentences with less repetition. You can often provide far less practice and maintain a far less strict criterion of performance. Occasionally, students will need firming, but they will tend to learn the sentences much faster than they do at first.

Word-Attack Exercises

General Information

The words the students are to read during the word-attack portion of the lesson appear in the textbook. The words are in columns, each containing four to six words.

The main purpose of the word-attack exercises is to teach students the new words that will appear in the stories and information passages they read. For words that students probably understand, there is no work on word meaning. For words that may be unfamiliar to the students, you'll tell the meaning of the word or show how to use the word in a sentence. The words that have a meaning emphasis are scattered throughout the lists. In the sample on the next page from lesson 46, there are four words for which you provide information about meaning. (Three are in column 1, one is in column 4.)

1	2	3
1. strength	1. sprayed	1. several
2. human	2. cleared	2. continue
3. mountain	3. cooled	3. corners
4. excitement	4. napped	4. hairy
5. California		5. enemy

4	5
1. Pacific Ocean	1. cross
2. globe	2. Japan
3. jet's	3. attention
4. free	4. closets
5. web	5. mean-looking
6. strip	6. moments

EXERCISE 2

Reading Words

Column 1

a. **Find lesson 46 in your textbook.** ✔
- Touch column 1. ✔
- (Teacher reference:)

1. strength	**4. excitement**
2. human	**5. California**
3. mountain	

b. Word 1 is **strength.** What word? (Signal.) *Strength.*
- Spell **strength.** Get ready. (Tap for each letter.) *S-T-R-E-N-G-T-H.*
- Your strength is how strong you are. A person who is stronger has more strength. Who has more strength, a child or a grown-up? (Signal.) *A grown-up.*

c. Word 2 is **human.** What word? (Signal.) *Human.*
- Spell **human.** Get ready. (Tap for each letter.) *H-U-M-A-N.*
- Humans are people. Here's another way of saying **There were many people in the woods: There were many humans in the woods.**

d. Word 3 is **mountain.** What word? (Signal.) *Mountain.*
- Spell **mountain.** Get ready. (Tap for each letter.) *M-O-U-N-T-A-I-N.*

e. Word 4 is **excitement.** What word? (Signal.) *Excitement.*
- When you are worked up and have trouble sitting still, you feel excitement.

f. Word 5 is **California.** What word? (Signal.) *California.*

g. Let's read those words again, the fast way.
- Word 1. What word? (Signal.) *Strength.*
- (Repeat for words 2–5.)

h. (Repeat step g until firm.)

Column 2

i. Find column 2. ✔
- (Teacher reference:)

1. sprayed	**3. cooled**
2. cleared	**4. napped**

- All these words end with the letters **E-D.**

j. Word 1. What word? (Signal.) *Sprayed.*
- (Repeat for words 2–4.)

k. Let's read those words again.
- Word 1. What word? (Signal.) *Sprayed.*
- (Repeat for words 2–4.)

l. (Repeat step k until firm.)

Column 3

m. Find column 3. ✔
- (Teacher reference:)

> 1. <u>sev</u>eral   4. <u>hair</u>y
> 2. <u>con</u>tinue   5. <u>en</u>emy
> 3. <u>corn</u>ers

- These words have more than one syllable. The first syllable is underlined.

n. Word 1. What's the first syllable? (Signal.) *sev*.
- What's the whole word? (Signal.) *Several*.
- If several people are meeting, could there be three people? (Signal.) *Yes*.
- Could there be four people? (Signal.) *Yes*.
- Could there be two people? (Signal.) *No*.
- Could there be a lot of people? (Signal.) *No*.

o. Word 2. What's the first syllable? (Signal.) *con*.
- What's the whole word? (Signal.) *Continue*.
- What do you do when you keep on working? (Signal.) *Continue working*.

p. Word 3. What's the first syllable? (Signal.) *corn*.
- What's the whole word? (Signal.) *Corners*.

q. Word 4. What's the first syllable? (Signal.) *hair*.
- What's the whole word? (Signal.) *Hairy*.

r. Word 5. What's the first syllable? (Signal.) *en*.
- What's the whole word? (Signal.) *Enemy*.

s. Let's read those words again.
- Word 1. What word? (Signal.) *Several*.
- (Repeat for: **2. continue, 3. corners, 4. hairy, 5. enemy.**)

t. (Repeat step s until firm.)

Column 4

u. Find column 4. ✔
- (Teacher reference:)

> 1. **Pacific Ocean**   4. **free**
> 2. **globe**   5. **web**
> 3. **jet's**   6. **strip**

v. Number 1. What words? (Signal.) *Pacific Ocean*.
- Is the Pacific Ocean on the **east** coast or the **west** coast of the United States? (Signal.) *West*.

w. Word 2. What word? (Signal.) *Globe*.
- A small model of Earth is called a globe. A globe is shaped like a ball.

x. Word 3. What word? (Signal.) *Jet's*.
- (Repeat for words 4–6.)

y. Let's read those words again.
- Number 1. What words? (Signal.) *Pacific Ocean*.
- Word 2. What word? (Signal.) *Globe*.
- (Repeat for words 3–6.)

z. (Repeat step y until firm.)

Column 5

a. Find column 5. ✔
- (Teacher reference:)

> 1. **cross**   4. **closets**
> 2. **Japan**   5. **mean-looking**
> 3. **attention**   6. **moments**

b. Word 1. What word? (Signal.) *Cross*.
- (Repeat for words 2–6.)

c. Let's read those words again.
- Word 1. What word? (Signal.) *Cross*.
- (Repeat for words 2–6.)

d. (Repeat step c until firm.)

Individual Turns

(For columns 1–5: Call on individual students, each to read one to three words per turn.)

The individual lists have different decoding emphases. In the previous sample, column 1 presents words that are difficult to decode. These words are modeled before students read them. The students also spell some of these words. (Note that students never spell more than four words per lesson.)

Columns 2 through 5 present decodable words that require no modeling. The words in column 2 have endings. Column 3 presents multisyllabic words. The first component in each word is underlined. The presentation for these words requires students to attend to the components. (First they read the underlined part of the word; then they read the whole word.) The words in columns 4 and 5 are miscellaneous, decodable words that will appear in the reading selections. For all these words you, (1) indicate the number of the word students are to read; (2) say What word?; (3) then signal. For example, for word 1 you say, Word 1. What word? When you say word 1, students are to touch under the word. When you say, What word? they are to say the word.

The arrangement and focus of the various columns change from one lesson to another. In some lessons, words that have a particular sound feature will be grouped in a column—for instance, words that have the letter combinations **ce** or **ge.** Students spell some words, but never more than four per lesson. Some lists focus on various types of multisyllabic words. Some lists focus on endings. And some lists have no particular focus except that the words will appear in an upcoming reading selection.

The amount of drill and practice that you provide should depend on how well students read selections. If their reading is accurate and fluent (students reading at close to a conversational rate and not generally exceeding the error limit), you can usually go through the word lists very quickly and with very little repetition. If there are some students in the group who are a little weak, give them more individual turns. But do not try to give all students individual turns.

Presenting Word-Attack Exercises

Maintain clear signals. Use a clap or some other *auditory* signal to indicate when the students are to respond. Your signal should follow the last word of the task by one second. The timing should always be the same—very rhythmical and predictable.

Correct signal violations early in the program. If the students do not respond on signal, tell them what they did or what they should do: Wait for the signal, or You're late. Then repeat the task, reinforcing the students if they respond on signal. Once you know that the students are firm, you can relax the corrections on signal violations, but don't let the students get so sloppy that you can't clearly hear their responses.

Correct droning, sing-song responses. Tell students, Say it the way you talk. Model the correct behavior and enforce it. Also, check your pacing and make sure you model responses in a normal speaking voice.

Confirm all words that are read correctly by the group. This is important early in the program. For example, immediately after the group reads the word **information,** say, Yes, **information.** This practice guards against the possibility that some students misread the word but that you didn't hear the misreading.

Correct all word-reading errors immediately. Even if only one student in the group makes an error, say the correct word.

Work within a specified time frame. The word-attack portion of the lesson takes more time on some days than on others. However, even in the longest lessons, *the word-attack portion should not take more than seven or eight minutes.*

Position yourself so you can observe what students are doing. If you are working with a large group of students, do not stand in front of the group as you present the word-attack exercises. Instead, walk among the students. When you stand behind them and look over their shoulders, you can see whether they are pointing to the appropriate words, and you can observe their responses better than if you are in front of them.

A good procedure is to focus on six to eight individual students. Stand behind one of them as you present two or three words. Then move behind another one. Select the students that probably would make mistakes. Observe whether they are:

- pointing to the appropriate words
- saying the correct words
- initiating the response on signal or waiting for others to lead them

Regular Reading Selections

Reading Mastery Signature Edition, Grade 2 presents two types of regular reading selections: main stories and story background passages. Virtually all regular lessons and fluency checkout lessons have a main story. Not all of these lessons have a story background passage. During the first half of the program, a story background passage appears in almost every regular lesson and fluency checkout lesson. In the second half of the program, story background passages are less frequent, occurring in about half the lessons.

A list of story background passages and main stories appears by lesson in Appendix F.

Story Background Passages

Story background passages are designed to prepare students for comprehending details of upcoming main stories. If a story contains information that students probably do not know, a story background passage precedes the main story. The comprehension passage is not as long as the main story, usually between 100 and 200 words. For example, a main story may refer to insects. Before students read this selection, they read a story background passage that gives them relevant information about insects.

If a story background passage appears in a lesson, it appears immediately before the reading of the main story. Here's the story background passage from lesson 41.

 Insects

Most bugs are insects. Some bugs are not insects.

An ant is an insect. A fly is an insect. A butterfly is an insect. A beetle, a bee, and a grasshopper are insects. Spiders are not insects.

Here are the rules about all insects:

• An insect has six legs.
• The body of an insect has three parts.

An ant has six legs. Its body has three parts. So an ant is an insect.

A fly has six legs. Its body has three parts. So a fly is an insect.

A spider has eight legs. Its body has two parts. So a spider is not an insect.

Main Stories

General Information

For main stories a word-decoding error limit is specified. The error limit for all main stories is based on two errors for each 100 words read aloud. The limits are designed so that students won't become anxious about reading and thus read hesitantly. At the same time, if students perform within the accuracy limits, they are accurately reading 98 out of 100 words.

The procedures for directing the reading of the story are spelled out in detail in the presentation book. Here is the format from lesson 15:

Story Reading

a. Find part C in your textbook. ✔
• We're going to read this story two times. First you'll read it out loud and make no more than 6 errors. Then I'll read it and ask questions.
b. Everybody, touch the title. ✔
• (Call on a student to read the title.) *[Goad the Toad.]*
• Everybody, what's the title? (Signal.) *Goad the Toad.* (ND)
c. (Call on individual students to read the story, each student reading two or three sentences at a time.)

• (**Correct errors:** Tell the word. Direct the student to reread the sentence.)
• (If the group makes more than 6 errors, direct the students to reread the story.)

---

d. (After the group has read the selection making no more than 6 errors:) Now I'll read the story and ask questions.

Goad the Toad

Once there was a toad named Goad. Goad was the biggest toad you have ever seen. Goad was bigger than a baseball. She was even bigger than a toaster.

• Everybody, show me with your hands how big a toaster is. ✔ (APK)
• Are there really toads that big? (Signal.) *No.* (APK)
• Real toads are about as big as my fist. So is Goad a real toad or a make-believe toad? (Signal.) *Make-believe toad.* (R/F)

Goad was not only big. She was smart. She was smarter than a trained seal. Not only was Goad big and smart, Goad was fast. She was faster than a cat chasing a mouse.

- We know three things about Goad. Let me read that part again. You listen and get ready to tell the three things:

  Goad was not only big. She was smart. She was smarter than a trained seal. Not only was Goad big and smart, Goad was fast. She was faster than a cat chasing a mouse.
- Everybody, Goad was big and smart and what else? (Signal.) *Fast.* (ND)

  Goad lived near a large lake called Four Mile Lake. It was four miles from one end of the lake to the other.

- Why was it called Four Mile Lake? (Call on a student. Idea: *Because it was four miles from one end to the other.*) (DC)
- The map shows Four Mile Lake. Touch the west bank of the lake. ✔
- There's a dotted line that goes through the lake. Follow that line and see how many miles you go before you reach the east bank. ✔
- Everybody, how many miles? (Signal.) *Four.* (VA)

  Goad liked to visit places on Four Mile Lake. Sometimes, she would hop over to the logs near the north shore of the lake.

- Everybody, touch the letter at the north shore of the lake in the picture. ✔
- What letter? (Signal.) *T.* (VA)

  Sometimes, she would hop over the hills on the south shore.

- Everybody, touch the letter at the south shore of the lake. ✔
- What letter? (Signal.) *B* (VA)

  Sometimes, she would go for a dip near the east shore of the lake.

- Everybody, touch the letter at the east shore of the lake. ✔
- What letter? (Signal.) *W.* (VA)

  When Goad was in the water, she was not fast. She could not swim as fast as a seal or a goldfish. In fact, she could not swim as fast as a very slow frog.

- Everybody, was Goad fast on land? (Signal.) *Yes.* (RF/R)
- Was she fast in water? (Signal.) *No.* (ND)

  When Goad was in the water, she looked like a floating pillow with two big eyes.
  Because Goad was so big, and so fast, and so smart, thousands of hunters went to Four Mile Lake every year to see if they could catch Goad.

- Why did they want to catch her? (Call on a student. Ideas: *Because she was different from the other toads; because she was so big, fast, and smart.*) (DC)

  People from the circus knew that if they had Goad, they could put on a show that would bring thousands of people to the circus.

- Would a great big smart toad make a good circus act? (Call on a student. Idea: *Yes.*) (MJ)

  Hunters from zoos knew that people would come from all over to visit any zoo that had a toad like Goad. Some hunters came because they wanted to become rich.

- How could they become rich by catching Goad? (Call on a student. Ideas: *Make people pay to see her; sell her to the zoo.*) (DI)

> Goad was worth thousands of dollars to anybody who could catch her. But nobody was able to catch her.
> MORE NEXT TIME

- Why do you suppose that nobody was able to catch Goad? (Call on a student. Ideas: *She was too smart; she was too fast*.) (MJ)

Overview of Story-Reading Procedures

The story-reading procedures change throughout the program. Here is a summary of the procedures.

Lessons 1–91: On the first reading, students read the **entire** story aloud. You call on individual students, each to read two or three sentences. You may ask some comprehension questions. These usually relate to predictions about what will happen in the story. On the second reading, **you** read the entire story and ask the remaining comprehension items.

Lessons 92–145: On the first reading, students read most of the story aloud. They do not read the last part of the story, however. You present some comprehension items. On the second reading, you read the same part of the story the students have read. You present comprehension items that relate to this part. Then students read the end of the story to themselves, and you present comprehension items for that part.

Presenting the Reading of Story Background Passages and Main Stories

Here are procedures for effectively directing the group reading of story background passages and main stories:

Make sure you receive a good sample of each student's reading behavior. For groups that have over 15 students, you may not receive adequate feedback about the performance of some students. The simplest remedy is to observe students reading individually during paired practice.

Make sure that students follow along as others are reading. Students are to point to the words that are being read. Pointing is a behavioral indication that those students who are not reading aloud are reading silently. Think of the pointing behavior as a way of maximizing practice. By pointing, the students practice reading throughout the group reading. If they don't point, they may practice only when they are reading aloud—a very scant amount of practice.

To ensure that students follow along, establish the procedure that students lose their turn if they don't have their place when they're called on.

If the group is large (over 15), circulate among the students and observe them from behind.

Decoding Errors in Main Stories

Each main story has an error limit. If students are placed appropriately, the group should regularly read within the error limit. Follow these guidelines for dealing with decoding errors:

Remind students of the error limit for the story and tell them how they are doing. Remember, we aren't going to make more than seven errors, so read carefully. Reinforce accurate reading: Good job. You're reading very carefully. Warn the students if they tend to make careless mistakes: The group has already made five errors, so be careful.

- If the students read within the error limit, congratulate them for doing a good job. Remind them that it is very hard: That was a tough story and this group read it making only __ errors. That's pretty good.

- If the students do not read within the error limit, (1) they are to reread the story, and (2) *you will ask no questions during this rereading.*

Try to schedule the rereading as soon as possible. If there is time in the period, start the rereading immediately. Typically, however, the rereading will have to be scheduled during the next reading lesson.

Tally each error and give immediate feedback. Here is a list of common decoding errors:

- *Omitting an ending.* Saying "look" for *looked* is an error. Saying "run" for *runs* is an error.

- *Saying the wrong word.* Saying "a" for *the* is an error. Saying "what" for *that* is an error.

- *Repeated self-corrections.* A self-correction occurs when a student says the wrong word and then rereads the word correctly before

you correct the student. If a student responds with the correct word after some signal has been given that the initial reading was wrong, count the self-correction as an error. If a student does a lot of self-correcting, count all self-corrections as errors. However, if the group makes only occasional self-corrections (no more than 1–3 per story), do not count them as errors.

- *Word omissions or insertions.* If a student reads *They went with the boys from town,* as "They went with the boys from **the** town," count the inserted word as an error. If a student reads the sentence as, "They went with boys from town," the omitted word should be counted as an error.

- *Repeated line skipping.* Like self-corrections, occasional line-skipping should not be treated as an error; simply tell the student to move up to the appropriate line and reread the entire sentence. However, if line-skipping occurs frequently, count each occurrence as one error.

- *Repeated partial readings.* If a student usually reads sentences in this manner: "They went with went with the boys from town," count one error. Occasional rereadings to fix the phrasing of the sentence are acceptable. Chronic rereadings, however, should be treated as errors.

- *Repeated word-part or syllable reading.* If a student usually pronounces longer words a part at a time before saying the word, the student is making decoding errors. Count each **chronic** occurrence of word-part or syllable reading as one error. For example, if the student reads "Ma— manu— manufac— manufacture," count one error.

Remember, the number of decoding errors will drop if you:

- give the students feedback on how they are doing.

- make sure that you are not letting errors pass.

- respond immediately to mistakes.

Correcting Decoding Errors During Selection Reading

There is only one procedure for correcting decoding errors during selection reading:

1. Stop the reader as soon as you hear the error.

2. Indicate whether the reader skipped a line, reread a word, omitted a word, or misread a word. For misread words, say the word and ask the student to repeat it: That word is _____. What word?

3. Direct the student to read the sentence from the beginning: Go back to the beginning of that sentence and read it again.

The last step is particularly important. The only way you know whether the correction was effectively communicated is that the student correctly reads the sentence in which the mistake occurred.

Recording Performance

The reproducible group summary chart that appears in Appendix H is designed for keeping track of:

- the group's performance on the reading of the main story;

- the performance of individual students on their five-lesson fluency checkouts;

- students' tenth-lesson test performance;

- students' independent work.

Each chart covers a ten-lesson span. The sample chart on the next page has been partially filled in for lessons 41 to 50.

The top of the chart provides the summary information for the group. You record the number of errors the group made in reading each main story. If the group exceeds the error limit, you circle the number. The 9 for lesson 45 is circled because the error limit for lesson 45 is 8.

Presenting Comprehension Activities

The presentation script for each main story and comprehension passage indicates the comprehension items you are to present.

Present items specified for the first reading and the second reading. Comprehension passages are read once, but most main stories are read twice. The text indicates both the items that are to be presented on each reading and when they are to be presented.

Teacher **Ms. Turner**   **Reading Mastery Signature Edition**   Group ___2___
Grade 2

Lessons	4 1	4 2	4 3	4 4	CO 4 5	4 6	4 7	4 8	4 9	CO/Test 5	
Main Story Errors	7	8	8	8	(9)	11	7	5	9		
Name	IW	IW	IW	IW	CO	IW	IW	IW	IW	IW	CO	Test
Luis Cepeda					/						/	
Yoko Higashi					/						/	
Anita Diaz					/						/	
Denise Barton					/						/	
Zachary Gray					/						/	
Eric Adler					/						/	
					/						/	

Items that are to be presented on the first (or only) reading are preceded by a small number 1.

Items that are preceded by a small number 2 are to be presented on the second reading. These appear only in the script for the main stories (not for comprehension passages, because there is no second reading for comprehension passages). All second-reading items are preceded by a small number 2.

The following sample is from lesson 119. The text in the screened boxes is the story the students read. After Toby says to himself, "What a shabby circus," on the first reading, you say, If it's a shabby circus, does it have a lot of good acts? After students read what Toby said to himself during the second reading, you do not present a comprehension item.

Some of the illustrations are reproduced in the script, and items immediately follow the illustration. For example, the script shows an illustration and some questions following the second reading of the sentence, "The rest of them were complaining." The items below the illustration refer to the illustration.

Story Reading

a. Find part C in your textbook. ✔

• The error limit for group reading is 10. Read carefully.

b. Everybody, touch the title. ✔

• (Call on a student to read the title.) *[Toby's New Job.]*

• Everybody, what's the title? (Signal.) *Toby's New Job.* (ND)

• Where did we leave Toby? (Call on a student. Idea: *In his cage at the circus.*) (APK)

• What time of day was it? (Call on a student. Idea: *Nighttime.*) (APK)

• How did Toby feel? (Call on a student. Ideas: *Sad; homesick.*) (APK)

c. (Call on individual students to read the story, each student reading two or three sentences at a time. Ask questions marked **1.**)

• **(Correct errors:** Tell the word. Direct the student to reread the sentence.)

• (If the group makes more than 10 errors, direct the students to reread the story.)

---

d. (After the group has read the selection making no more than 10 errors, read the story to the students and ask questions marked **2.**)

Toby's New Job

The next morning, the circus owner came and took Toby from his cage. The owner said, "You are going to do tricks for the people who have come to see our circus. If you want to eat, you will do tricks. If you do <u>not</u> do tricks, you will become a <u>very</u> hungry animal."

Toby said, "Oh, bad and super bad."

1. Why would Toby become a very hungry animal if he does not do tricks? (Call on a student. Idea: *Because the circus owner wouldn't feed him.*) (DI)

1. Do you think he'll do tricks for the circus owner? (Call on individual students. Student preference.) (P)

The owner took Toby into a tent. In the middle of the tent was a ring.

"What a shabby circus," Toby said to himself.

1. If it's a shabby circus, does it have a lot of good acts? (Signal.) *No.* (DC)

This circus did not have many animals and people doing super things. Toby was the only animal in the tent. The owner was dressed up in a black suit with a rip in the back of the coat.

There was no huge crowd of people watching the act. There were about twenty people sitting in the stands. Three of them were sleeping. Two of them were little kids who were crying. The rest of them were complaining.

2. The picture on the next page shows the shabby circus.

2. Touch the circus owner. ✔ (VA)

2. Look at the rip in the back of his suit.

2. Everybody, about how many people are in the stands? (Signal.) *20.* (ND)

2. Touch somebody who is sleeping. ✔ (VA)

One girl said, "We want to see lions and tigers."

"Yeah," somebody else said. "We don't want to see a dumb kangaroo."

The owner held up his hands. "This kangaroo can do tricks that will surprise you. This kangaroo is the smartest kangaroo in the world. People usually pay as much as a hundred dollars to see this kangaroo perform."

2. Everybody, is the circus owner telling the truth? (Signal.) *No.* ⓓⓒ

"Boo," the people yelled. "We want lions."

Then a girl yelled, "Make that kangaroo ride a bicycle."

"Make him ride it backward," a boy yelled.

The other people began to clap. "Yes, let's see him ride a bicycle backward."

"Wouldn't you rather see him being shot from a cannon?" the owner asked.

"No," the people agreed. "We want to see that kangaroo ride a bicycle backward."

The owner tried to argue with the crowd, but when people started to throw things at him, he said, "All right, he will ⭐ ride a bicycle backward."

2. At first the circus owner argued with the crowd. What did he want to do to Toby? (Call on a student. Idea: *Shoot him from a cannon.*) ⓃⒹ

2. Everybody, did the crowd agree with the circus owner? (Signal.) *No.* ⓃⒹ

2. So did the circus owner finally agree to have Toby ride a bicycle backward? (Signal.) *Yes.* ⓃⒹ

The owner got a dusty bicycle. He held up one hand and said to the crowd, "Ladies and gentlemen. Today the Kankan Circus presents Toby, the wonder kangaroo. Toby will amaze you by riding a bicycle backward. And he will do this

amazing trick on a high wire ten meters above the floor."

2. Where is Toby supposed to ride the bicycle? (Call on a student. Idea: *On a high wire 10 meters above the floor.*) ⓃⒹ

Toby looked up at the wire ten meters above the floor. You know what Toby said.

1. Say what he probably said. (Call on a student. Idea: *Oh, double bad.*) Ⓟ

The owner handed Toby the bicycle and said, "Take this bicycle up the ladder. Then ride it backward on the high wire."

Toby shook his head, no.

The owner said, "<u>Do</u> it, you bad kangaroo. Get up there and ride that bicycle."

Toby shook his head, no.

The owner turned to the crowd. "Before Toby, the wonder kangaroo, rides the bicycle on the high wire, he will ride it backward on the floor."

2. The circus owner changed the announcement because Toby wouldn't do it on the high wire.

The owner turned to Toby. "Ride that bicycle on the floor."

Toby shook his head, no.

People were beginning to throw things at Toby and the owner. "This is a rip-off," they were hollering. "That kangaroo can't do anything."

The owner said, "One moment, ladies and gentlemen. Before Toby rides the bicycle backward on the floor, Toby will ride it forward on the floor."

The owner looked at Toby and said, "Do it." Toby shook his head, no.

> People were now yelling, "I want my money back," and "Let's call a cop."

1. Go back to the beginning of the story. Follow along while I read.
2. What was the last thing the owner wanted Toby to do? (Signal.) *Ride the bicycle forward on the floor.* (ND)
2. Is it easier to ride **forward** or **backward?** (Signal.) *Forward.* (APK)
2. Read the rest of the story to yourself. Find out two things. First find out what Toby was supposed to do before he rode the bicycle forward on the floor. Then find out what two boys in the crowd did. Raise your hand when you're done.

> The owner held up his hands and said, "Before Toby rides the bicycle forward on the floor, Toby will walk with the bicycle on the floor."
> Toby looked at the owner and shook his head no again.
> "This is the worst show in the world," people were yelling. A woman was shaking her umbrella at the owner. Two boys were throwing papers at Toby. Toby was saying, "Oh, worse than bad."
> MORE NEXT TIME

2. (After all students have raised their hand:) What was Toby supposed to do before he rode the bicycle forward on the floor? (Call on a student. Idea: *Walk with the bicycle on the floor.*) (ND)
2. Everybody, is he going to do that? (Signal.) *No.* (ND)
2. What were two boys in the crowd doing? (Call on a student. Idea: *Throwing papers at Toby.*) (ND)
2. Raise your hand if you remember what Toby said as the boys threw papers at him. (Call on a student.) *[Oh, worse than bad.]* (ND)
2. That must be the worst circus in the world.

Do not become sidetracked into long discussions. Certainly you may present additional tasks; however, these should be infrequent. For example, if the students have had problems with a particular name or concept, it's all right to add a task even though the script does not indicate an item. If a specified task asks for student opinions, do not poll the entire group. A couple of quick responses will suffice.

Use the wording indicated in the script. Tasks that begin with the word *everybody* call for a group, unison response. Tasks that say *Call on a student* are to be presented to a single student. Tasks that are followed by *Call on individual students* call for a range of responses. In some cases, the task will call for an opinion, such as: What do you think will happen? In other cases, the students are asked to name items that fall into a particular category: Name some animals that are warmblooded.

Accept appropriate ideas for tasks that are answered by an individual. The appropriate response for the first task (Where did we leave Toby?) is expressed as an idea. (Idea: *In his cage at the circus.*) An appropriate response is one that clearly expresses this **idea,** regardless of the specific words used in the response— *at a shabby circus, in a run-down circus.* Present a follow-up task if the response is not sufficiently specific. For example, if a student responds "in a cage," you would say, Where was that cage?

Use a real globe of the world to present those tasks that specify a globe. These tasks appear in lessons 39, 46–48, 51, 113, 132, 135, and 139. Make sure that you have a globe available. Do not try to use a flat map instead of a globe. The concepts that are conveyed through the presentation of the globe are critical. If you don't present them as specified, a large percentage of students will not learn these concepts and will fail a host of review items that assume a basic understanding of the globe.

Reducing Comprehension Errors

If the students make a mistake on an oral comprehension task, correct the error, mark the task, and tell them: I'm going to ask that question later. So remember the answer. At the end of the story, present any marked tasks. If an individual turn was missed, present the task to an individual (not necessarily the same one who missed the task).

Correcting Comprehension Errors During Selection Reading

You will correct two types of tasks: tasks in which students have just read the passage that answers the questions and tasks in which the information was presented earlier.

For each type of correction, you will follow this general pattern:

1. Make sure students have the information they need to answer the question.

2. Repeat the task.

3. Repeat the task again at a later time.

For different item types, there are corresponding variations of this correction.

- If the passage the students just read answers the question, reread the passage or summarize the content before repeating the task the students missed.

- If the passage students just read does not answer the question, you will tell the students the information they need to answer the question before you repeat the task.

- If the passage does not give the answer and if further facts will not clarify the answer, you tell them the answer, then repeat the task.

When information is presented in the passage students just read, you make sure they have the information they need either by rereading the passage or by telling them the relevant information. Sometimes, you'll be able to give them the information they need by asking them a series of questions. If you can't think of good questions to ask, however, you can simply tell them the information they need.

Example: Why would Toby become a very hungry animal if he does not do tricks? A student responds, *"He wouldn't eat enough,"* which is possibly correct. You ask, But why wouldn't he eat enough? The student fails to answer.

1. **Repeat the part that answers the question:** Listen to that part again: The owner said, "You are going to do tricks for the people who have come to see our circus. If you want to eat, you will do tricks. If you do <u>not</u> do tricks, you will become a <u>very</u> hungry animal."

2. **Repeat the task:** Why would Toby become a very hungry animal if he does not do tricks?

3. **Give the correct answer, if necessary:** If the student doesn't respond appropriately, say, The **owner** wouldn't feed him.

4. **Remind the students that you'll repeat the task at a later time:** Remember that answer. I'm going to ask the question later. At a later time, repeat the question.

When not all information is presented in the passage students just read, you tell students the information they need.

Here's the correction for a mistake from lesson 117. The item involves knowledge of Pip's show-off behavior.

Example: Why would Pip like to stand in the bright sun? The student responds, "I don't know."

1. **Refer to information presented earlier:** Does Pip think he is beautiful? *Yes.*

   Can people see how beautiful he is if there's not much light? *No.*

2. **Repeat the task:** Why would Pip like to stand in the bright sun?

3. **Give the correct answer, if necessary:** Because the sunlight will show off his feathers.

4. **Repeat the task at a later time.**

At the end of the period, or at another time the group members are present (after recess, just before lunch, etc.) ask the students questions they missed. Remember to give them enough story information for them to answer the question.

When additional facts do not clarify the answer:

1. **Tell students the answer.**

2. **Repeat the task.**

3. **Repeat the task at a later time.**

Note that these items usually ask "Why?" or require students to make a judgment or draw a conclusion. Here's an example from lesson 117: Why would the sailors want to hide the animals? A student responds, *"I don't know."*

Here's the correction:

1. **Tell the student the answer:** They don't want the police to know that they have animals like peacocks and kangaroos on the ship.

2. **Repeat the original task:** Why would the sailors want to hide the animals?

3. **Remind the students that you'll repeat the task at a later time.**

Correcting Errors on Picture Tasks

Some picture tasks require students to touch an illustration or operate on it in some way. The task may be, Touch that path, or Touch the steam rising from the pond. These tasks are presented to the group, but are not accompanied by a signal to respond. Responses are incorrect if students:

- copy responses produced by a neighbor

- touch the wrong object

- fail to respond

- give ambiguous responses

To correct picture mistakes, show the students the right response. If possible, repeat the task later.

Example: The picture shows objects being drawn to a whirlpool. The task is: Touch object C and trace the path it will take. The mistake: A student points in a vague manner above the page or does not clearly trace the path. The correction: Put your finger right on the page. Touch point C. Now follow the dotted line and show me the way the object will move. Do not accept ambiguous responses.

Some picture tasks require students to observe details of pictures and produce **verbal** responses about these details. Treat these verbal responses the same way you would treat responses to a written question. The picture answers the question you ask, so you would tell students the answer, repeat the task, and possibly repeat it later (although it may be difficult to do this without the book).

Here's an example from lesson 39.

What is C? *Copilot.*

Correction:

1. **You tell the answer:** It's a flight attendant.

2. **You repeat the task:** What is C?

3. **Later you can ask students a question that is like the one you presented.**

Paired Practice

General Information

Following the main-story reading, students work in pairs and reread part of the story. Each student reads about 200 words. Students are permanently assigned. Partners are to sit next to each other. They can either read from the same text or from two texts. Allow 5 minutes for paired practice.

Possible Problems

Here are the more common problems teachers encounter when implementing paired-practice procedures:

1. Students take too long to get started.

2. Students take too long to complete the reading.

3. Students become lax about following along when they are not reading and therefore do not respond to the partner's errors.

For problem 1: The simplest way to get students into the reading faster is to have a structured beginning. One good plan is to require some sort of response for the pair—such as both partners sitting next to each other with books in place and raising their hands. They are not to start reading until you acknowledge that they have raised their hands.

It's time for paired practice. Raise your hand when you and your partner are ready.

Acknowledge each pair and tell them to start.

Praise students who start quickly, That was a good start. Almost all the teams are ready to read.

If some partners consistently take more than a few seconds to get ready for the paired practice, reassign the members of the team, or place a stronger contingency on getting started on time.

For problem 2: Set up a reinforcing contingency for completing the reading in a reasonable amount of time. If students often take 8 minutes to complete the reading, set the time limit at 7 minutes and give students who perform within this time limit praise and possibly some other reinforcer. After students consistently read within 7 minutes, change the time limit to 6 minutes.

For problem 3: Monitor the students as they read and have students report on their partner's errors.

If students are not catching errors their partners make, require the checker to write the number of errors the partner made.

At the end of the paired practice, record a quick summary:

A team, raise your hand if your partner made no errors.

Raise your hand if your partner made 1 or 2 errors.

Raise your hand if your partner made more than two errors.

Summarize the results on the board. Then conclude, Well, it looks like the B team won today, but not by much. We'll see who wins next time.

The system works because the students want their team to win. If students miss their partner's errors, however, the partner's team gets an advantage.

Independent Work

General Information

As part of every lesson, the students work independently for about 20 to 30 minutes, completing all the textbook items specified for that lesson as well as completing side 1 and side 2 of that lesson's worksheet.

Here are the types of items students work:

- Items based on the story background passage read that day (only on lessons that have a story background passage);

- Items based on the main story in the lesson;

- Skill items (sequencing, deductions, vocabulary review, alphabetizing, etc.);

- Review items based on information from earlier lessons (either from story background passages or main stories);

In addition, students independently write sentences. This work is part of a 10-minute spelling period that occurs at another time of day. (See **Spelling Lessons,** page 72.)

Early Preparation

During the first part of the program, the teacher reads the items.

- Lessons 1–5. The teacher reads all independent work items aloud. After reading each item, the teacher calls on a student to answer the item. The teacher corrects mistakes and repeats items that students miss.

- Lessons 6–9. After the main story, individual students read and answer all items except review items.

- Lessons 11–15. After the main story, students orally read items for the story background passage and the main story but do not answer them aloud. The teacher introduces new types of skill items.

- Lessons 16–35. After the main story, students orally read only the main story items. The teacher continues to introduce new types of skill items.

- Lessons 36–145. As a rule some items appear in the textbook and some on the worksheets. The teacher does not read items, with the exception of specific skill items. When new types of skill items are introduced, the teacher goes over them with the students.

Observe Students as They Work Independently

Plan to observe the group at work on the independent-work activities every few lessons, especially during the first 20 lessons.

Identify specific problems students have. Make sure they are on task and are not copying from each other. Serious problems should be corrected immediately.

Is the student reading items correctly?
As part of answering correctly, students must read items correctly. Often it is possible to infer how a student misread an item from the response. For example, an item reads, "Why was Toby happy when he saw the police boat?" The student answers, "Yes." Inference: The student read the item as "Was Toby happy when he saw the police boat?" Tell the student: I don't think you read that item carefully. Read it again.

Note: As a rule, you shouldn't help a student more than once during a lesson. The more you help, the less information you have about what a student actually knows, and the more the student will rely on you for help.

Is the student working at a reasonable rate? Students who are just learning how to work independently often don't use their time well. They need feedback about how much time has passed and how they are performing.

A good tactic is to remind the students about their rate of performance. As you observe different students, make positive comments to the group about different students' rates: Oh, here's somebody who's already finished the workbook items. Very good . . . Here's somebody else who is almost that far along. Fantastic.

If the students tend to go slowly, make sure you give students feedback about how they are doing as they work. For example, after they have worked for about fifteen minutes, remind them that they should have finished about half the independent work assignment.

Help students who get "stuck" on a particular item. They may not have a strategy for completing the exercises and then returning to problem items. Explain the strategy of (1) circling the number of a problem item, (2) skipping that item and working all non-problem items, and (3) returning to the problem (circled) item.

Are the answers to items correct? Refer to the answer key. If the answer a student wrote is not correct, tell the student something like: Your answer to item 5 is not correct. You should not tell the student the answer, and usually you should not provide more than one of these prompts to each student per lesson.

Answers that are obviously correct present no problem. But you may have questions about answers that have grammatical errors, that do not correspond precisely to the answer given in the answer key, or that contain misspelled words.

Some of the answers in the key are labeled "Idea." This designation means that the student's response must give a correct answer; however, the students are not required to use the exact words that appear in the key. The reason these items are shown as having "idea" answers is that there are different ways of expressing the answer, and all answers that express the idea are equally correct.

Here's an item with some responses that students wrote. Item: Why did the Vikings like Tom and Eric's dog?

In the selection, their dog growled at a woman, and defeated the Viking's best dog.

Below is the answer key for this item:

11. Why did the Vikings like Tom and Eric's dog?

Ideas: Because it was a good fighter; because it was mean.

A response that expresses **either** of these ideas would be correct. Below are responses students wrote. Some of these answers are clearly correct or incorrect. Others present problems. You can test the items by asking yourself, Do I know what the student is trying to say? Did the student use enough words to really say that? Can I overlook any wording misuse and still judge that the student expressed the idea?

1. *He won their best dog.* Clearly, the student means he **beat** their best dog. The problem is usage. The student expressed the idea. The answer is correct.

2. *It beat the other dog.* This answer has no problems. It clearly expresses the idea and uses adequate wording.

3. *To fight with dogs.* The answer is wrong. It does not answer the question: Why did the Vikings like their dog? Furthermore, the item does not express the idea that their dog won the fight.

4. *It fought the dog.* The answer is probably wrong, but you might give it the benefit of the doubt. The Vikings were impressed by the skill of the dog, not by the mere fact that it fought. However, you could argue that it takes courage to fight.

5. *It was mad.* The answer is clearly wrong. The student may be trying to say, "It was mean," but **mad** and **mean** are not close enough, and we can't overlook the difference because the word **mad** is the only clue we have about what the student is trying to say.

6. *It was fast.* The answer is clearly wrong. (The story mentioned that the dogs were the same size but that Tom and Eric's dog was faster. However, the story gave no indication that the Vikings were impressed by the speed, but rather by the victory.)

7. *It did not stop.* The answer is wrong.

Do students spell the words correctly? Here are some rules about spelling errors for **words that are not spelling words**:

1. If the word appears in the item, it should be spelled correctly in the answer.

2. If the word does not appear in the item, it will not be counted wrong if it is spelled incorrectly.

If *down* is a spelling word, the students could be held accountable for it. However, don't try to identify every spelling word students should know. Spot-check items as you monitor the students. If you notice spelling words that are misspelled, mark them, but focus primarily on the words in the item. If the answers have words that appear in the item, the words should be spelled correctly.

Are the answers to *how* and *why* questions expressed appropriately? Some students do not write appropriate answers to these questions. For instance, the item, "Why did he go to the library?" is appropriately answered, "To get a book," or

"Because he wanted a book," or "He wanted a book." Some students, however, may write, "A book." That answer is unacceptable.

To correct this type of response, present items orally. Then direct students to write appropriate answers.

Note that when students answer the questions orally, they tend to answer them correctly. For example:

Listen: Why did he go to the library?

To get a book.

Yes, **to get a book.** Those are the words that answer the question. Say those words.

To get a book.

Write them.

Present tasks like the previous one until students are very firm on the words they are to write.

Remedies for students who can't remember story information. Starting with lesson 36, the basic procedure is for students to complete their independent work without first hearing items read or answered. Students are supposed to remember the information from reading the story and answering the oral comprehension items (which usually include all the written items they will respond to).

If some students have great difficulty remembering the information from the story and continue to make mistakes on independent work because they don't recall the answers, you may introduce a temporary procedure:

- Direct students who have problems remembering the information to write answers to all the items they can work.

- Next, have them circle the number of any items they cannot answer.

- Direct them to read these items to themselves.

- Tell them, Remember the questions that are circled because you'll look in your story to find the answers.

- Permit them to look at their story one time to find answers to all items. Students are not to write anything during the time they are looking in the story. Also, students are to limit their information search to the lesson that was read today. They are not to refer to earlier selections.

  Pencils down. You may look at today's story one time to find answers you couldn't remember. You have three minutes. You have to find answers to all your questions in three minutes. You can't write anything until you're done reading.

- Monitor students and make sure that they do not write the answer to one question and then attempt to look at the story again. Remind them, You can only look at the story one time.

Repeat the procedure on no more than 12 lessons. Remind students that they should try to remember the answers when the story is being read by the group. Reinforce students who improve in remembering information.

Workchecks

General Information

The goal of the workcheck is to review the independent-work tasks and to make sure that (1) students are not making too many errors and (2) students learn the correct answers to items they miss. The workcheck is not mere paper marking. It is teaching. It is particularly important for *Reading Mastery Signature Edition,* Grade 2 because many items will appear as review items on later lessons. Some students will miss these items repeatedly unless you present daily workchecks.

The independent work consists of the worksheet pages for the lesson and answers to textbook items written on lined paper.

During the workcheck, you go over all the items and students mark all items that are wrong.

At the end of the workcheck students record the total number of errors they made at the top of the lined paper. Students change all incorrect answers and hand in their lined paper and their worksheet (side 1 and side 2).

You quickly spot-check the worksheet answers and those on lined paper. Don't spot-check only items that had mistakes, because some students are not reliable about marking incorrect answers.

After the spot-check, you will use the Group Summary Chart to record the number of errors each student made on the lesson. (See **Recording Errors,** page 57.)

A "passing grade" for each lesson is three or fewer errors. This criterion is fairly stiff because many lessons call for 35–40 responses. The structure of the program makes it possible for most students to pass almost all lessons. The record of errors may be used to award grades. More importantly, the error performance indicates how well the students are performing, what they are mastering, and whether they need additional practice.

The workchecks are designed to provide that practice and to assure that students continue to perform well in the lessons.

A workcheck is most efficiently handled as a group activity. It should be conducted some time after the group has completed the independent work activities, but before the next lesson is presented.

Although details of the procedure may vary from situation to situation, here are things you should do during the daily workcheck:

- Check the written responses to all items. (Answer keys for worksheet and textbook items appear in the Answer Key book.)

- Make sure that all incorrect responses are marked with an **X.**

- Give the students information about correct answers to items, so they can later change their incorrect answers.

- Make a final check of each student's written work after the student has changed all the incorrect answers.

- Then record the number of errors (the number of items originally marked with an X and later corrected).

The workcheck should not take a great deal of time. In most cases, it requires only six to nine minutes. If it takes much longer, (a) your pacing is too slow, or (b) the students are not firm in some skills that are important in completing the independent work. Work on both possibilities.

Presenting Workchecks

Students may check their own independent work during the workcheck. They should use a colored pencil for checking.

The fastest procedure for going through the workcheck is for you to **read each item and call on a student to tell the correct answer.** Students who have questions may raise their hand. If many students have questions about a particular item, tell them to mark the item with a question mark. Go quickly to the next item.

As you read the items and give the answers, circulate among the students. Make sure they are marking each incorrect response with an **X.** By circulating among the students, you will discourage the students' tendency to change their answers without first marking the item as incorrect.

Firm items that a lot of students tend to miss, and firm students who consistently make more than three errors on their independent work. You firm by giving additional practice.

There are different formats for firming, but the simplest is for you to go over the items

that many students miss and provide paired practice for students who tend to make too many errors.

For example, some students tend to have trouble with measurement units—inch, centimeter, meter, yard. Plan to firm the group by having them use their hands to show you an inch, a yard, etc. Take a minute or two at the end of the workcheck and present the task, Everybody, show me a space that is about an inch . . . Show me a space that is about a meter and so forth. If students tend to copy the responses of others, direct them to keep their eyes closed during the tasks. Close your eyes and show me a space that is about a foot . . . Open your eyes. You should have a space about this wide . . .

Don't try to firm all difficult items in one setting. Instead, give students short bursts of practice (10–15 trials) in possibly three or four lessons.

For students who consistently make three or more errors, provide paired practice. Pair the lower students with students who do well on the independent work. The higher student presents the various items the other student missed and gives feedback on each answer. The paired practice could be scheduled for about five minutes a lesson (possibly at the end of the workcheck period).

Plan to firm students on sets of related facts—particularly geographic information and time-line information. In both cases, some students confuse similar facts. (Students are often naive about dates; however, they are required to learn quite a few dates.)

The simplest format is like the fact-review, a sample of which appears below.

FACT REVIEW

a. Let's review some facts you have learned.
First we'll go over the facts together. Then I'll call on different students to do some facts.

b. Everybody, tell me when Eric and Tom were in the Land of the Vikings. (Pause.) Get ready. (Signal.) *1000.*
- Tell me when Eric and Tom were in San Francisco. (Pause.) Get ready. (Signal.) *1906.*
- Tell me when Eric and Tom were in the city of the future. (Pause.) Get ready. (Signal.) *4000 years in the future.*
- Tell me when the United States became a country. (Pause.) Get ready. (Signal.) *1776.*
- (Repeat step b until firm.)

c. Tell me when Greece and Troy went to war. (Pause.) Get ready. (Signal.) *3000 years ago.*
- Tell me when Eric and Tom were in Egypt. (Pause.) Get ready. (Signal.) *5000 years ago.*
- Tell me when Columbus discovered America. (Pause.) Get ready. (Signal.) *1492.*
- Tell me when Eric and Tom were in Concord. (Pause.) Get ready. (Signal.) *1777.*
- (Repeat step c until firm.)

Individual Test

- Now I'm going to call on each of you to do some facts. (Call on each student to do the facts in one step.)

The review consists of three or four items that students tend to confuse and two or three items that generally give students no trouble.

You may use this format for geography items, measurement items, or any group of items that students tend to confuse.

If students make a lot of mistakes on independent work, direct them to redo either the entire page on which the errors occurred, or just the part that presented problems.

Recording Errors

Record errors for independent work for the students *after* you have looked at their corrected work. The number of independent-work errors has been written by the students at the top of the lined paper (at the end of the workcheck). Check the numbers for accuracy. Record the number of errors in column **IW** of your Group Summary Chart.

The sample Group Summary Chart on the next page has been filled out for lessons 41 through 49. The shaded areas show the parts of the chart used for recording independent-work errors.

A passing grade for each lesson is three or fewer errors. Yoko Higashi's **IW** performance for lesson 41 is circled, indicating that a remedy is needed.

It is important to monitor students' independent work performance. If students start making a large number of errors on their independent work, firm them before proceeding in the program.

Teacher **Ms. Turner**   *Reading Mastery Signature Edition*   Group **2**
Grade 2

Lessons	4 1	4 2	4 3	4 4	CO 4 5		4 6	4 7	4 8	4 9	CO/Test 5	
Main Story Errors	7	8	8	8	(9)		11	7	5	9		
Name	IW	IW	IW	IW	CO	IW	IW	IW	IW	IW	CO	Test
Luis Cepeda	2	1	2	1		2	1	0	1	3		
Yoko Higashi	(4)	3	2	2		2	3	1	2	2		
Anita Diaz	1	1	1	0		2	1	1	0	2		
Denise Barton	1	2	0	1		1	0	1	0	2		
Zachary Gray	1	0	0	1		1	2	1	1	1		
Eric Adler	2	1	1	0		1	0	1	0	2		

Fluency: Rate/Accuracy

General Information

During every fifth lesson, starting with lesson 10, each student receives an individual fluency checkout. In these lessons that end with the digit 5 (15, 25, etc.), the paired practice is deleted. Students therefore have time for the individual fluency checkouts. The average time available for individual fluency checkouts is about fifteen minutes.

Fluency checkouts take about a minute-and-a-half per student. If the group is large, you may need an additional checker. You may use an aide, an older student, a parent volunteer, or possibly a higher-performing student in the classroom. The main qualification for a checker is the ability to identify reading errors and keep accurate time. If an additional checker is not available, you may be able to finish the checkouts at some later time in the school day. Possibly, you could finish them during the next lesson.

Each fluency checkout is conducted by an aide, adult volunteer, or by the teacher.

To conduct fluency checkouts, the checker calls up individual students as the group works on independent-work activities. The student orally reads a specified passage from the main story of the preceding lesson. For example, for the fluency checkout in lesson 30, each student reads a specified passage from lesson 29. The passage in the student textbook has marks at the beginning and at the end (✿).

The checker times each student. **To pass the checkout, the student must read the**

passage in one minute or less and make no more than two errors.

Conducting Fluency: Rate/Accuracy Checkouts

Identify a part of the room where a student can read individually to you or to the assigned checker. The simplest procedure is for the checker to:

- Sit next to the student.
- Tell the student when to begin reading.
- Observe the text that the student reads.
- Make a tally mark on a sheet of paper for each error.
- Help if the student gets stuck on a word for more than two seconds.
- Record the time it takes the student to complete the passage.

Decoding errors consist of word misidentifications, word omissions, line-skipping, and word additions. (Self-corrects and rereading words also may be counted as errors. See page 41.)

Note that the checker is not to correct errors unless the correction is necessary for the student to keep reading the passage. If the student can't read a word within about two seconds, the checker says the word and marks it as an error. The checker may first ask, "Do you want me to tell you the word?"

Student's Records

Each student keeps a record of reading checkout performance with thermometer charts (reproducible copies of which are at the back of student workbooks and in Appendix J of this guide). During the program, the student will fill in three thermometer charts. Together, they show all the reading checkouts the student passed.

- The current thermometer charts may be posted in the classroom, kept in individual student folders, or in a central folder that you keep.

- If a student passes a checkout on the first trial, the student colors the appropriate space of the thermometer red. For example, if the student passes the checkout for lesson 35, the student colors the space for 35 red.

- If the student passes the checkout, but not on the first trial, the student colors the appropriate space, but not red. You may use blue, black, pink, or some other color.

When the student completes *Reading Mastery Signature Edition,* Grade 2, all three thermometer charts should be completely filled in. The colors show whether the student needed additional firming, and where that firming occurred.

Recording Rate-and Accuracy Performance

Use column **CO** on the Group Summary Chart to record the number of errors each student made and whether the student passed (**P**) or failed (**F**) the rate criterion (one minute or less).

The **CO** columns on the Group Summary Chart have two parts. Record **P** or **F** in the top half of the box to indicate whether the student **passed** or **failed** the rate criterion. Record the student's number of decoding errors in the bottom half of the box.

The sample Group Summary Chart on page 61 has been filled out for lessons 41 through 50. The shaded columns show the parts of the chart used to record rate and accuracy performance for the individual fluency checkouts in lesson 45 and lesson 50 (test 5). Note that Denise Barton's **CO** performance for lesson 45 is circled, indicating that a remedy is needed.

Firming Students Who Do Not Pass Fluency Checkouts

The students who do not pass a fluency checkout on their first attempt should reread the passage aloud until they achieve an acceptable rate-accuracy performance. During these readings, students should be told which words they missed. After each reading, they should study the passage and then reread that passage to the checker.

Students who don't pass two consecutive attempts to meet the rate-accuracy criterion for a checkout should receive additional oral-reading practice.

- This practice should be modeled after the fluency checkouts, with the exception that the student who is reading should receive immediate feedback about words that are misread. The checker simply tells the correct word.

- A plan that works well is to direct the student to read the last two or three stories that the group has read. Use the same error limit that is specified for group reading.

Teacher Ms. Turner   **Reading Mastery Signature Edition** **Group** 2
Grade 2

Lessons	4 1	4 2	4 3	4 4	CO 4 5		4 6	4 7	4 8	4 9	CO/Test 5	
Main Story Errors	7	8	8	8	⑨		11	7	5	9		
Name	IW	IW	IW	IW	CO	IW	IW	IW	IW	IW	CO	Test
Luis Cepeda	2	1	2	1	P/0	2	1	0	1	3	P/0	
Yoko Higashi	④	3	2	2	P/0	2	3	1	2	2	P/1	
Anita Diaz	1	1	1	0	P/0	2	1	1	0	2	P/0	
Denise Barton	1	2	0	1	Ⓕ/1	1	0	1	0	2	P/2	
Zachary Gray	1	0	0	1	P/0	1	2	1	1	1	P/0	
Eric Adler	2	1	1	0	P/1	1	0	1	0	2	P/1	

- Monitor the student's paired-reading practice. Make sure that the student is participating and the partner is responding to any mistakes the reader makes. If the practice is not adequate, either reassign the student to another partner or increase the amount of paired-reading practice the student receives.

Often, the student who is weak in decoding will tend to make a greater number of errors when tackling long passages. Therefore, the checker can take turns with the student, the checker reading one paragraph (or a few lines) and the student reading the next few lines.

A good variation is for the checker to read somewhat haltingly and make mistakes from time to time. The student is to catch these mistakes. By reading haltingly, the checker ensures that the student will be

able to follow along. Requiring the student to catch the checker's mistakes ensures that the student is attending to the words even when not reading aloud. The periods during which the checker reads are therefore not merely "breaks." They are a switch from one kind of accuracy performance to another.

Fact Games

General Information

Fact games occur every tenth lesson as part of the test lessons, starting with lesson 30. The game is presented before the test. Fact games give students a great deal of practice with facts and rule applications. The games are important because many oral tasks presented during the regular lessons are answered by individuals, not by the whole group, which means that the students may not receive sufficient practice with many tasks.

Some facts are particularly troublesome for many students. The games provide intensive practice on these facts, but do so in a context that is reinforcing. The games become a combination of work and fun.

Groups of four players and a monitor play the game. (More than one group can play simultaneously.) Each group has a question sheet (or sheets) with 11 items numbered 2 through 12. The teacher reproduces these Fact Game sheets from blackline masters located in Appendix G.

To take a turn, a player rolls two dice (or number cubes). The player then adds the numbers on the cubes together, reads the item that corresponds to that number total (2 through 12), and responds to the item (which may involve answering several questions).

An assigned student monitor refers to the answer key in the back of the textbook and indicates whether the answer is correct. If so, the player earns a point and a checkmark is made on the student's scorecard. After 10 minutes, direct all students who earn more than 10 points to stand up.

On the next page is the fact game from lesson 90 and scorecard 90.

Reproducible Fact-Game scorecard sheets appear at the back of each workbook and at the back of this guide. Each student needs a copy for lessons 30 through 140.

Introducing the First Fact Game

The instructions for the first game (lesson 30) specify that you will be the monitor and demonstrate with four players how the game is played. When demonstrating the game, make sure that you model fast pacing, correct procedures, and appropriate responses to the players.

After demonstrating a few "rounds" of the game, assign students to permanent groups. Ideally, a group should consist of four players and a monitor. In some situations, you may have to form a group that consists of three or five players and a monitor. If possible, try to avoid larger groups. Each player in a larger group will receive fewer turns, and managing the group becomes more difficult.

Do not make groups homogeneous. (Do not place the better performers in one group and the lower performers in the other.) Rather, mix students of varying ability.

Assign monitors who are competent. The monitors should be good readers. Tell the monitors their responsibilities. They are to make sure that the players are taking turns, moving to the left. The monitor directs the player who is taking a turn to read the item aloud and answer it. Then the monitor confirms a correct response or gives the correct answer if the item was missed.

The next player does not roll the cubes until the preceding player has answered and has been told whether the response is correct. (If players are permitted to roll before the item is read and answered, they become so intent on getting ready for their turn that they do not listen to the preceding player's item and the answer.)

2. a. Which army was Achilles in during the war between Troy and Greece?

    b. How long was he in the war?

    c. Who won when he fought against Hector?

3. a. Who was the greatest soldier of Troy?

    b. Achilles rode around the wall of Troy in a ▇▇▇.

4. a. Name a good place to look for clues about people who lived long ago.

    b. Tell when eohippus lived.

5. As you touch each horse, say the letter. Then name the horse.

6. a. Things closer to the top of the pile went into the pile ▇▇▇.

    b. Things closer to the bottom of the pile went into the pile ▇▇▇.

Lesson 90

1	2	3	4	5
6	7	8	9	10
11	12	13	14	15
16	17	18	19	20

The fact game items appear on blackline masters (Appendix G near the back of this guide). Make one copy of the game for each group. Give each group two dice or number cubes.

The answers for the fact games appear at the back of the textbook.

Here are the procedures for playing:

- The monitor is the only person in a group who is permitted to look at the answer page.

- The other players take turns. A player rolls the cubes, adds the numbers showing, reads the item that has the same number, and tells the answer.

- If the player answers correctly, the monitor makes one tally mark in the box at the top of the player's question sheet. Or the monitor says, "Correct," and the player then makes one tally mark.

- The cubes go to the next player (the player to the left), and that player takes a turn.

Here are procedures for setting up the groups:

- If possible, provide a table for each group of players. There should be no obstructions that would prohibit the monitor from observing the players. Players should not be seated directly next to the monitor (where they could read the answers in the monitor's book).

- Each player's scorecard sheet should be on the table, ready for the game.

- If the monitor is to tally each player's correct answers, the monitor should have a pencil. If the monitor is to direct the players to make the tally marks, each player should have a pencil. **Note:** It is important that their scorecards are visible so the monitor can see whether the players are tallying correctly.

Observing the Fact Games

Follow these guidelines when you observe the games.

Reinforce a fast pace. Praise players who have the number cubes ready to roll, find the item quickly, read it correctly, and answer correctly. Remind the players that the faster they play, the more points they can earn. A fast pace also ensures that the players will be less likely to argue with the monitor.

Make comments about each group's progress: Look at how well you're doing. You've already played three rounds. Comments of this type are important because they let the students know that they are part of a group that is working together.

Do not permit the games to drag. If the groups are going slowly, tell the monitor, Come on, let's get this game moving. Nobody's going to earn very many points if they are this slow. A more positive, effective technique is to comment on games that are moving quickly: Wow, this group is really moving. Every player has had five turns already.

Make sure that players are following the rules. After the players have played the game for a few minutes, they may remember what item 5 is or what item 3 is. Therefore, they may attempt to answer the item without first reading the item aloud. For example, they'll say, "Number 3. San Francisco," rather than reading the item, "What place does the letter E show?" Stop players who do not read the item aloud, and remind them of the rule: You must *read* the item aloud and *then* answer it. This stipulation is very important. Many items are included in the game because they are difficult for the students. The difficulty will be reduced greatly if a strong association between the item and the answer is established. This association is ensured, however, only if the students read the item aloud before answering it. Although the students may read it accurately to themselves, the other students in the group will not receive the benefit of hearing the item *and* the answer.

Make sure monitors award points only when the answers are correct. For nearly all items, the correct response is phrased in a very specific way, which is indicated in the answer key.

Unless the player's response is the same as that in the key, the response is incorrect. (There are a few items in later games that permit players to express an idea. For those items, the monitor must use some judgment. For most items, however, very little judgment is required.)

If an answer is not correct, the monitor is to read the correct answer aloud. Students are not permitted to argue with the monitor. If they argue, they lose a turn. The monitors are to raise their hand to signal a problem or a question they can't answer.

Stop the game after it has been played for 10 minutes. When only three minutes of playing time remain, tell the groups: Only 3 minutes more. When the time limit is up, tell the groups to stop: If a player has started a turn, finish that turn. Then the game is over.

Tell each group of players how well they did. Announce which groups played the game smoothly. Tell all students who have more than 10 points to stand up. Congratulate them.

Test lessons occur every ten lessons, beginning with lesson 10. Each test consists primarily of content introduced and practiced in the preceding nine lessons. The tests also assess skill items and the vocabulary sentences that students have practiced.

In every test lesson students also do an individual fluency checkout. Starting with lesson 30, students play a fact game before taking the test.

Test lessons that have both a written test and fluency reading checkout provide you with detailed performance information about individuals and about the group. The test shows you how well individuals and the group comprehend the content that was presented in the different selections, and also shows how well students perform on the skills and vocabulary being taught. The individual fluency checkouts give information about how accurately and fluently students read. This package of information permits you to identify specific problems that individual students have, identify problems that are common to more than one student, and provide timely remedies.

Administering the Tests

1. Make sure that students have all materials they need: lined paper, textbook, and pencil.

2. Seat students so they cannot see the work of other students.

3. Direct students to complete the test and turn it in.

4. Score and grade the tests, and perform any necessary remedies before presenting the next lesson.

Scoring the Tests

There are different formats for marking the test, one of which is to perform a workcheck, during which students use a **marking pencil** to indicate which items are wrong (with an **X**). A variation is a workcheck in which students exchange tests and mark each others' tests. A third (and preferable) alternative is for you to score each test.

Even if you do not score each test, you should go over every test and make sure that the marking is accurate. After checking each student's test, write the total number of errors at the top of the test.

Recording Test Performance

You should record each student's performance in two places—on the Group Summary Chart (Appendix H) and on the Test Summary Sheet (Appendix I). A copy of the Test Summary Sheet for tests 1–8 appears below.

You record each student's performance by circling the number of each item the student missed. If the student missed items 3 and 18, you circle the numbers 3 and 18 for that student. The passing criterion for each test is shown at the bottom of the column for each test. Note that the criteria are not the same for different tests. (The criterion for test 2 is 20 correct out of 22, but the criterion for test 5 is 30 correct out of 33.) If the student fails the test, write **F** over the box with item numbers, or circle the box. Either system gives you a quick visual summary of the students who passed versus those who had trouble. In the Test 5 sample on page 69, Denise Barton has a failing score (29 correct out of 34 with passing criterion of 31/34) and so her box has been circled.

TEST SUMMARY SHEET

Name	Test 1	Test 2	Test 3	Test 4	Test 5	Test 6	Test 7	Test 8
	1 2 3 4 5 6 7 8 9 10 11 12 13 14 15 16 17 18 19 20 21 22 23 24	1 2 3 4 5 6 7 8 9 10 11 12 13 14 15 16 17 18 19 20 21 22	1 2 3 4 5 6 7 8 9 10 11 12 13 14 15 16 17 18 19 20 21 22 23 24 25	1 2 3 4 5 6 7 8 9 10 11 12 13 14 15 16 17 18 19 20 21 22 23 24 25 26	1 2 3 4 5 6 7 8 9 10 11 12 13 14 15 16 17 18 19 20 21 22 23 24 25 26 27 28 29 30 31 32 33	1 2 3 4 5 6 7 8 9 10 11 12 13 14 15 16 17 18 19 20 21 22 23 24 25 26 27 28 29 30 31 32	1 2 3 4 5 6 7 8 9 10 11 12 13 14 15 16 17 18 19 20 21 22 23 24 25 26 27 28 29 30 31 32 33 34 35 36	1 2 3 4 5 6 7 8 9 10 11 12 13 14 15 16 17 18 19
	1 2 3 4 5 6 7 8 9 10 11 12 13 14 15 16 17 18 19 20 21 22 23 24	1 2 3 4 5 6 7 8 9 10 11 12 13 14 15 16 17 18 19 20 21 22	1 2 3 4 5 6 7 8 9 10 11 12 13 14 15 16 17 18 19 20 21 22 23 24 25	1 2 3 4 5 6 7 8 9 10 11 12 13 14 15 16 17 18 19 20 21 22 23 24 25 26	1 2 3 4 5 6 7 8 9 10 11 12 13 14 15 16 17 18 19 20 21 22 23 24 25 26 27 28 29 30 31 32 33	1 2 3 4 5 6 7 8 9 10 11 12 13 14 15 16 17 18 19 20 21 22 23 24 25 26 27 28 29 30 31 32	1 2 3 4 5 6 7 8 9 10 11 12 13 14 15 16 17 18 19 20 21 22 23 24 25 26 27 28 29 30 31 32 33 34 35 36	1 2 3 4 5 6 7 8 9 10 11 12 13 14 15 16 17 18 19
	1 2 3 4 5 6 7 8 9 10 11 12 13 14 15 16 17 18 19 20 21 22 23 24	1 2 3 4 5 6 7 8 9 10 11 12 13 14 15 16 17 18 19 20 21 22	1 2 3 4 5 6 7 8 9 10 11 12 13 14 15 16 17 18 19 20 21 22 23 24 25	1 2 3 4 5 6 7 8 9 10 11 12 13 14 15 16 17 18 19 20 21 22 23 24 25 26	1 2 3 4 5 6 7 8 9 10 11 12 13 14 15 16 17 18 19 20 21 22 23 24 25 26 27 28 29 30 31 32 33	1 2 3 4 5 6 7 8 9 10 11 12 13 14 15 16 17 18 19 20 21 22 23 24 25 26 27 28 29 30 31 32	1 2 3 4 5 6 7 8 9 10 11 12 13 14 15 16 17 18 19 20 21 22 23 24 25 26 27 28 29 30 31 32 33 34 35 36	1 2 3 4 5 6 7 8 9 10 11 12 13 14 15 16 17 18 19
	1 2 3 4 5 6 7 8 9 10 11 12 13 14 15 16 17 18 19 20 21 22 23 24	1 2 3 4 5 6 7 8 9 10 11 12 13 14 15 16 17 18 19 20 21 22	1 2 3 4 5 6 7 8 9 10 11 12 13 14 15 16 17 18 19 20 21 22 23 24 25	1 2 3 4 5 6 7 8 9 10 11 12 13 14 15 16 17 18 19 20 21 22 23 24 25 26	1 2 3 4 5 6 7 8 9 10 11 12 13 14 15 16 17 18 19 20 21 22 23 24 25 26 27 28 29 30 31 32 33	1 2 3 4 5 6 7 8 9 10 11 12 13 14 15 16 17 18 19 20 21 22 23 24 25 26 27 28 29 30 31 32	1 2 3 4 5 6 7 8 9 10 11 12 13 14 15 16 17 18 19 20 21 22 23 24 25 26 27 28 29 30 31 32 33 34 35 36	1 2 3 4 5 6 7 8 9 10 11 12 13 14 15 16 17 18 19
	1 2 3 4 5 6 7 8 9 10 11 12 13 14 15 16 17 18 19 20 21 22 23 24	1 2 3 4 5 6 7 8 9 10 11 12 13 14 15 16 17 18 19 20 21 22	1 2 3 4 5 6 7 8 9 10 11 12 13 14 15 16 17 18 19 20 21 22 23 24 25	1 2 3 4 5 6 7 8 9 10 11 12 13 14 15 16 17 18 19 20 21 22 23 24 25 26	1 2 3 4 5 6 7 8 9 10 11 12 13 14 15 16 17 18 19 20 21 22 23 24 25 26 27 28 29 30 31 32 33	1 2 3 4 5 6 7 8 9 10 11 12 13 14 15 16 17 18 19 20 21 22 23 24 25 26 27 28 29 30 31 32	1 2 3 4 5 6 7 8 9 10 11 12 13 14 15 16 17 18 19 20 21 22 23 24 25 26 27 28 29 30 31 32 33 34 35 36	1 2 3 4 5 6 7 8 9 10 11 12 13 14 15 16 17 18 19
	1 2 3 4 5 6 7 8 9 10 11 12 13 14 15 16 17 18 19 20 21 22 23 24	1 2 3 4 5 6 7 8 9 10 11 12 13 14 15 16 17 18 19 20 21 22	1 2 3 4 5 6 7 8 9 10 11 12 13 14 15 16 17 18 19 20 21 22 23 24 25	1 2 3 4 5 6 7 8 9 10 11 12 13 14 15 16 17 18 19 20 21 22 23 24 25 26	1 2 3 4 5 6 7 8 9 10 11 12 13 14 15 16 17 18 19 20 21 22 23 24 25 26 27 28 29 30 31 32 33	1 2 3 4 5 6 7 8 9 10 11 12 13 14 15 16 17 18 19 20 21 22 23 24 25 26 27 28 29 30 31 32	1 2 3 4 5 6 7 8 9 10 11 12 13 14 15 16 17 18 19 20 21 22 23 24 25 26 27 28 29 30 31 32 33 34 35 36	1 2 3 4 5 6 7 8 9 10 11 12 13 14 15 16 17 18 19
	1 2 3 4 5 6 7 8 9 10 11 12 13 14 15 16 17 18 19 20 21 22 23 24	1 2 3 4 5 6 7 8 9 10 11 12 13 14 15 16 17 18 19 20 21 22	1 2 3 4 5 6 7 8 9 10 11 12 13 14 15 16 17 18 19 20 21 22 23 24 25	1 2 3 4 5 6 7 8 9 10 11 12 13 14 15 16 17 18 19 20 21 22 23 24 25 26	1 2 3 4 5 6 7 8 9 10 11 12 13 14 15 16 17 18 19 20 21 22 23 24 25 26 27 28 29 30 31 32 33	1 2 3 4 5 6 7 8 9 10 11 12 13 14 15 16 17 18 19 20 21 22 23 24 25 26 27 28 29 30 31 32	1 2 3 4 5 6 7 8 9 10 11 12 13 14 15 16 17 18 19 20 21 22 23 24 25 26 27 28 29 30 31 32 33 34 35 36	1 2 3 4 5 6 7 8 9 10 11 12 13 14 15 16 17 18 19
	1 2 3 4 5 6 7 8 9 10 11 12 13 14 15 16 17 18 19 20 21 22 23 24	1 2 3 4 5 6 7 8 9 10 11 12 13 14 15 16 17 18 19 20 21 22	1 2 3 4 5 6 7 8 9 10 11 12 13 14 15 16 17 18 19 20 21 22 23 24 25	1 2 3 4 5 6 7 8 9 10 11 12 13 14 15 16 17 18 19 20 21 22 23 24 25 26	1 2 3 4 5 6 7 8 9 10 11 12 13 14 15 16 17 18 19 20 21 22 23 24 25 26 27 28 29 30 31 32 33	1 2 3 4 5 6 7 8 9 10 11 12 13 14 15 16 17 18 19 20 21 22 23 24 25 26 27 28 29 30 31 32	1 2 3 4 5 6 7 8 9 10 11 12 13 14 15 16 17 18 19 20 21 22 23 24 25 26 27 28 29 30 31 32 33 34 35 36	1 2 3 4 5 6 7 8 9 10 11 12 13 14 15 16 17 18 19
Passing Criterion	22/24	20/22	22/25	23/26	30/33	29/32	32/36	17/19

Teacher **Ms. Turner**   *Reading Mastery Signature Edition*   Group _____**2**_____
Grade 2

Lessons	4 1	4 2	4 3	4 4	CO 4 5	4 6	4 7	4 8	4 9	CO/Test 5	
Main Story Errors	7	8	8	8	(9)	11	7	5	9		
Name	IW	IW	IW	IW	CO	IW	IW	IW	IW	IW	CO	Test
Luis Cepeda	2	1	2	1	P/0	2	1	0	1	3	P/0	2
Yoko Higashi	(4)	3	2	2	P/0	2	3	1	2	2	P/1	2
Anita Diaz	1	1	1	0	P/0	2	1	1	0	2	P/0	0
Denise Barton	1	2	0	1	(F)/1	1	0	1	0	2	P/2	(5)
Zachary Gray	1	0	0	1	P/0	1	2	1	1	1	P/0	0
Eric Adler	2	1	1	0	P/1	1	0	1	0	2	P/1	2
					/						/	

You should also record each student's test performance on the Group Summary Chart. In the **Test** column, write the number of errors each student made on the test. Circle any number that exceeds the passing criterion for the test.

The sample Group Summary Chart above has been filled out for lessons 41 through 50 (test 5). The shaded column shows the part of the chart used for recording test 5 performance. (Denise Barton missed 5 out of 34 items. Her failing score has been circled.)

Test Remedies

Reproducible blackline masters of the Test Summary Sheets appear in Appendix I. The Test Summary Sheets provide an item-by-item analysis of the errors each student made. This information implies the kind of remedies that should be provided (ideally before you present the next lesson). A sample Test Summary for test 5 has been filled out and appears on the next page.

Total Errors

The total errors a student made tells you whether the student is progressing adequately. Students who exceed the specified number of errors are not performing at a level required to thoroughly comprehend the material they read.

Error Patterns

The basic patterns that you should look for when summarizing the data are: (a) a student (or groups of students) who fails the passing criterion on two or more consecutive tests; (b) the same item (or group of related items) being missed by more than 1/4 of the students.

Test Summary Sheet

Name	Test 5
Luis Cepeda	1 2 3 4 5 6 7 8 9 10 11 12 13 14 15 <u>16</u> 17 <u>18</u> 19 20 21 ㉒ 23 ㉔ 25 26 27 <u>28</u> 29 30 31 32 33 34
Yoko Higashi	1 2 3 4 5 6 7 8 9 10 11 12 13 14 15 16 17 <u>18</u> 19 20 <u>21</u> 22 23 ㉔ 25 26 ㉗ <u>28</u> 29 30 31 32 <u>33</u> 34
Anita Diaz	1 2 3 4 5 6 7 8 9 10 11 12 13 14 15 16 17 18 19 20 21 22 23 24 25 26 27 28 29 30 31 32 33 34
Denise Barton	1 2 3 4 5 <u>6</u> 7 8 9 <u>10</u> 11 ⑫ 13 14 15 ⑯ 17 <u>18</u> <u>19</u> 20 21 ㉒ 23 24 ㉕ 26 <u>27</u> <u>28</u> 29 30 31 32 �33 34
Zachary Gray	1 2 3 4 5 6 7 8 9 10 11 12 13 14 15 16 17 18 19 20 21 22 23 24 25 26 27 28 29 30 31 32 33 34
Eric Adler	1 2 3 4 5 6 7 8 9 10 11 12 13 <u>14</u> 15 <u>16</u> 17 18 19 ⑳ 21 ㉒ 23 24 25 <u>26</u> 27 <u>28</u> 29 30 31 32 33 34
	1 2 3 4 5 6 7 8 9 10 11 12 13 14 15 16 17 18 19 20 21 22 23 24 25 26 27 28 29 30 31 32 33 34
	1 2 3 4 5 6 7 8 9 10 11 12 13 14 15 16 17 18 19 20 21 22 23 24 25 26 27 28 29 30 31 32 33 34
Passing Criterion	31/34

Students Who Fail Consecutive Tests

Any student who fails consecutive tests is probably misplaced in the program.
If more than one or two students exhibit this pattern, there are probably problems with the way the material is being presented, reviewed, and firmed. The first step in remediation would be to make sure that the students are trying. The simplest way is to provide them with some sort of reward or positive response for meeting the criterion on tests. For example, make a chart that shows the number of students who pass each test. Have a party or some special award for students who pass two or more consecutive tests. Also make sure that you have a solid workcheck and that students are doing the fact games.

In some cases, you will have students who do not really belong in the program—based on their reading performance—and there is no possibility of putting them in another group. Although you teach carefully, these students still do not perform at criterion. The best practice in this case is to do what you can in firming these students and providing additional practice **outside the regular reading periods.** But when you are teaching the reading group, do not gear the rate of the presentation to these students. Rather, gear it to the students who are appropriately placed in the program. If you gear the presentation to the students who are misplaced, you will go far too slowly for the others, and the presentation will be boring.

Students Who Fail the Same Items

If 1/4 or more of the students fail the same item or group of related items, those items require more practice and review. Here are the remediation steps.

1. Identify the common items that are missed, and create a fact review that involves these items.

A Test Firming Table for each test appears in the teacher presentation book, at the end of the test lesson. You may use this table to help you construct fact reviews (or to firm specific concepts). The table lists the test items and indicates the first lesson in which that item appeared. Here is the table for test 5.

Test 5 Firming Table

Test Item	Introduced in lesson	Test Item	Introduced in lesson	Test Item	Introduced in lesson
1	41	12	46	23	48
2	41	13	46	24	48
3	41	14	49	25	48
4	42	15	49	26	46
5	42	16	49	27	41
6	42	17	49	28	45
7	44	18	49	29	37
8	44	19	41	30	37
9	44	20	44	31	45
10	46	21	44	32	41
11	46	22	44	33	41

According to the Test 5 summary sample on page 69, 1/4 of the students missed items 9 and 19.

9. When a plane flies from New York City to San Francisco, is it flying in the **same direction** or the **opposite direction** as the wind?

19. What's the boiling temperature of water?
   • 212 miles   • 112 degrees   • 212 degrees

By checking the Test 5 Firming Table, we see that item 9 was introduced in lesson 44, and item 19 in lesson 41.

Now create a fact review that involves these items. (See page 58 and **Note** below.)

2. Present the fact review as part of the test remedy and then as part of subsequent lessons.

3. Present the items until the students are quite firm—virtually flawless.

4. If the number of students who had difficulties is large, present the review to the entire reading group.

Note: If students miss skill items or vocabulary items, you can follow a similar procedure in making up a fact review. For example, if students have trouble identifying what somebody said in sentences, you could say different sentences, and direct students to say what the person said. For example:

"My, my," she said. "What a nice day."
Tell me everything the girl said.

If students have trouble with deductions, present the first part of different deductions and direct students to say the conclusion. For example:

Fish live in water. A mackerel is a fish. So . . .

Sometimes, the trend is predictable. If there has been a substitute for several lessons before the test, the students probably will perform more poorly than they would if you had been working with them. The remedy is not only to go over the information that relates to the items the students tended to miss, but also to go over information that is closely related. For example, if students tend to miss three items about the nervous system, they would probably miss other items about the nervous system that were not on the test. Go over the independent work for the lessons that introduce the nervous system, and identify all key items. (The Test Firming Table in the teacher presentation book indicates the key lessons where items are introduced.) Present those items in a fact-review format. (This review is probably best presented to the entire reading group, not to only those students who had serious problems.)

Use a variation of the same procedure if the pattern occurs on material that you had presented. Sometimes students get overloaded with information. First see if the items they miss are related. If they are, refer to the independent-work items, and identify all the major facts that are related to the items the students missed. Present those facts in a fact-review format.

Retesting Students

After you have provided remedies, a general rule is to **retest students who failed.**

Do not retest the students after you simply mark answers on their test. Provide a remedy first. Before retesting make sure that they can respond correctly to the various items they missed. One purpose of the retest is to document that the remedy has worked. Another is to show the students that they can perform well on the tests and to provide them with the practice they need to achieve mastery.

Grades

The purpose of letter or number grades is to show the progress and skill level of the students. If students pass the tests consistently, and generally do not make more than three errors on their independent work, they deserve an A. The number grade would be over 90.

A student should be able to fail one or two tests and still earn an A. The reason is that some tests present difficult items.

The simplest grading system is to use the letter grades of A and F or U (for unsatisfactory). If students tend to meet criterion on independent work and tests, they receive an A. Otherwise, they receive a letter that suggests they are not performing adequately. Awarding Bs and Cs is difficult because the passing criteria for tests and independent work are quite high (sometimes above 90%). Students who average much below 90% are not performing adequately. If students do not meet the passing criteria for worksheets and tests, their percentage of correct responses may still be in the 80% range, but they are not performing at the level of mastery that is required by the program.

Spelling Lessons

Present the spelling component of *Reading Mastery Signature Edition,* Grade 2 at a time other than the period for reading. In other words, don't allow spelling lessons to infringe upon the time you've scheduled for reading. Each spelling lesson takes about ten to fifteen minutes, so you can use these lessons flexibly during the time allotted for language arts instruction. Spelling instruction begins with lesson 1 of the reading program and matches each reading lesson through 145. (You present Spelling lesson 1 on the same day as Reading lesson 1.) Remember, reading lessons match with spelling lessons, so under no circumstances should you end up on a spelling lesson beyond the reading lesson you are teaching.

Although these spelling lessons, when taught to mastery, will markedly improve your students' spelling ability, their greatest value might be that of reinforcing reading. The ability to *encode* a word strengthens students' ability to decode.

Material

You present lessons from the *Reading Mastery Signature Edition,* Grade 2 *Spelling Presentation Book.* Your students write answers for some activities on their own paper. They will need a red pen on test day.

How the Spelling is Taught

Follow the same conventions and critical teaching practices for teaching the spelling lessons that you use for teaching the reading lessons. As in a reading lesson, utilize group responses, clear signals, and fast pacing.

See the *Reading Mastery Signature Edition,* Grade 2 *Spelling Presentation Book* for further information.

Administering the Placement Test

As a rule of thumb, students who have successfully completed *Reading Mastery Signature Edition,* Grade 1 or a first grade reading program should be able to succeed in *Reading Mastery Signature* Grade 2. However, this rule may not apply to all students, particularly those who can decode words silently but cannot read aloud with sufficient accuracy (no more than two errors per hundred words). Also, students who are extremely weak in answering written comprehension questions should not go into *Reading Mastery Signature Edition,* Grade 2 or *Reading Mastery Signature Edition,* Transition.

The reproducible Placement Test on page 76a determines the rate-accuracy and comprehension performance of students. Administer the test to all students before placing them in *Reading Mastery Signature Edition,* Grade 2 or *Reading Mastery Signature Edition,* Transition. The test results will provide you with:

- "baseline" information about students' reading rate and accuracy.

- a basis for gauging the progress of students who are prepared to begin Grade 2.

- a means of identifying students who need the additional instruction and practice provided by Transition and those who should be placed in a Grade 1 sequence.

Instructions

- Make a copy of the blackline master of the Transition Placement Test (page 76a) for each student.

- Part 1 of the test consists of ten vocabulary words and a reading passage. The vocabulary word reading is not scored. The reading passage contains 159 words and is timed and scored.

- Part 1 of the test is to be administered individually to the students. They should not observe others taking the test. Part 1 requires about three minutes per student. You will need a stopwatch.

- Part 2 of the test may be presented to all the students at the same time. Part 2 requires the students to write answers to comprehension questions about the part 1 passage. Students have two minutes to complete part 2.

Test Administration Directions

Part 1—Vocabulary Word Reading (Not Scored)

a. (Call a student to a corner of the room, where the test will be given.)
b. (Give a copy of the test to the student.)
- (Teacher reference:)

1. **expert**	7. **difference**
2. **clinic**	8. **mirror**
3. **interest**	9. **through**
4. **changes**	10. **practicing**
5. **themselves**	11. **questions**
6. **people**	

c. (Point to the column of words at the top of the test. Tell the student:) Touch word 1. (Pause.) That word is **expert.**

d. (Repeat step c for words 2–10.)

e. Your turn to read those words.

f. Word 1. What word?
 • (Repeat for words 2–10.)

g. (Repeat step f until firm.)

Part 1—Passage Reading

h. (Point to the passage in part 1.)

i. (Tell the student:) You're going to read this passage out loud. I want you to read it as well as you can. Don't try to read it so fast that you make mistakes. But don't read it so slowly that it doesn't make any sense. You have three minutes to read the passage. Go.

j. (Time the student. If the student takes more than three seconds on a word, say the word, count it as an error, and permit the student to continue reading. Make one tally mark for each error.)

Count each of the following behaviors as an error:

• Misreading a word

• Omitting a word part

• Skipping a word

• Skipping a line (Immediately show the student the correct line.)

• Not identifying a word within three seconds (Tell the word.)

Also count each word not read by the end of the three-minute time limit as an error. For example, if the student is 8 words away from finishing the passage by the end of the time limit, count 8 errors.)

k. (Collect the test sheets.)

Criteria for Part 1

• Students who make 5 or fewer errors and read the passage in two minutes or less should proceed to part 2 of this test.

• Students who make fewer than 8 errors or read the passage between 2:01 and 3:00 minutes do not proceed to part 2 of this test. These students should be placed in the *Reading Mastery Signature Edition,* Transition program.

• Students who make 8 or more errors should be placed in the Grade 1 sequence or in a reading program with comparable decoding skills.

Part 2—Story Items

For students who have met the criteria, present part 2, which is a group test. Administer part 2 no more than two hours after students complete part 1. Here are the steps to follow:

a. (Assemble the students.)

b. (Give each student a copy of the placement test.)

c. (Give the group these instructions:) Follow along as I read the passage you read earlier.

　Bill tried to say things that would interest other people. He asked questions and tried to get people to talk about themselves. He said things that were funny. He talked faster and louder. He tried to smile more when he talked. But all those changes made no difference. After Bill was through speaking, everybody else was sleeping.

One day, Bill was at home. He was practicing in front of the mirror. He smiled, moved around a lot, and talked to the mirror.

Just then the door bell rang. Bill opened the door and saw a woman who said, "I am an expert at making people sleep. I work for the Sleep More Clinic. We help people who have trouble sleeping. I hear that you can make people sleep, too."

"Yes," Bill said. "If I speak for a while, people will sleep."

"That is interesting," the sleep expert said. "Can you explain why people sleep?"

"Yes, I can," Bill said.

(After reading the passage, say) At the bottom of the page are questions about the passage. Read the questions to yourself. Write or underline the answers. You have two minutes to finish.

d. (Time the students. Collect the test sheets after two minutes.)

Answer Key   Part 2

1. What was the first name of the man in the story? _____**Bill**_____

2. Underline 4 things he did to try to be more interesting.

- frown more
- <u>smile more</u>
- whisper
- <u>ask questions</u>
- answer questions
- <u>talk louder</u>
- talk softer
- <u>talk faster</u>
- talk slower

3. His problem was that he
- was old
- had five dogs
- <u>put people to sleep</u>

4. He practiced in front of
- his wife
- <u>the mirror</u>
- the TV

5. Who came over when he was practicing?
- a sleeper
- a dog expert
- <u>a sleep expert</u>

6. Name the place where she worked.

_____**Sleep More Clinic**_____

Scoring Criteria for the Placement Test

All students who made more than 8 errors on part 1 of the Placement test should be placed in the Grade 1 sequence or in a program that teaches comparable decoding skills.

Students who **should** be placed in the Transition program and begin instruction on Lesson 1 meet one of the following criteria on the Placement Test:

- Students who made fewer than 8 errors on part 1 and read the passage between 2:01 and 3 minutes.

- Students who made 6 or 7 errors on part 1 and read the passage in 2 minutes or less.

- Students who made 5 or fewer errors on part 1 and read the passage in 2 minutes or less and made 2 or more errors on part 2.

Students who made 5 or fewer errors on part 1, read the passage in 2 minutes or less and made 1 or no errors on part 2 should be placed in the Grade 2 sequence and begin instruction on Lesson 1. These students can also be placed in the Transition program if necessary.

The following table shows the placement criteria for the Placement Test:

Performance			
Errors Part 1	Time Part 1	Errors Part 2	Placement
8 or more	3 minutes or less	NA	Grade 1
Fewer than 8	2:01 to 3 minutes	NA	Transition
6 or 7	2 minutes or less	NA	Transition
5 or fewer	2 minutes or less	2 or more	Transition
5 or fewer	2 minutes or less	1 or 0	Grade 2 OR Transition

The following table shows the words per minute students read for specific times and numbers of errors on part 1 of the Placement Test.

	Errors								
Time	0	1	2	3	4	5	6	7	8
3:00	53	53	52	52	52	51	51	51	50
2:50	56	56	55	55	55	54	54	54	53
2:40	60	59	59	59	58	58	57	57	57
2:30	64	63	63	62	62	62	61	61	60
2:20	68	68	67	67	66	66	66	65	65
2:10	73	73	72	72	72	71	71	70	70
2:00	80	79	79	78	78	77	77	76	76
1:50	87	86	86	85	85	84	83	83	82
1:40	95	95	94	94	93	92	92	91	91
1:30	106	105	105	104	103	103	102	101	101
	Words per minute								

Part 1

1. expert
2. clinic
3. interest
4. changes
5. themselves
6. people
7. difference
8. mirror
9. through
10. practicing
11. questions

Part 2

1. What was the first name of the man in the story?

_____

Bill tried to say things that would interest other people. He asked questions and tried to get people to talk about themselves. He said things that were funny. He talked faster and louder. He tried to smile more when he talked. But all those changes made no difference. After Bill was through speaking, everybody else was sleeping.

One day, Bill was at home. He was practicing in front of the mirror. He smiled, moved around a lot, and talked to the mirror.

Just then the door bell rang. Bill opened the door and saw a woman who said, "I am an expert at making people sleep. I work for the Sleep More Clinic. We help people who have trouble sleeping. I hear that you can make people sleep, too."

"Yes," Bill said. "If I speak for a while, people will sleep."

"That is interesting," the sleep expert said. "Can you explain why people sleep?"

"Yes, I can," Bill said.

2. Underline 4 things he did to try to be more interesting.

• frown more   • talk louder
• smile more   • talk softer
• whisper   • talk faster
• ask questions   • talk slower
• answer questions

3. His problem was that he

• was old • had five dogs • put people to sleep

4. He practiced in front of

• his wife • the mirror • the TV

5. Who came over when he was practicing?

• a sleeper • a dog expert • a sleep expert

6. Name the place where she worked.

_____

PROJECT	PRESENT AFTER LESSON	MATERIALS
Map of Four Mile Lake	23	Large sheet of butcher paper or poster board (at least 5 feet x 4 feet), colored marker, scissors, construction paper, possibly paints or crayons, paste
Experiment of water's skin	35	Steel wool (preferably without soap), a transparent bowl, water, and several steel objects, like a wrench, screw or nails
Globe of Earth	52	Large plastic beachball (at least 18 inches in diameter), scissors, paste or tape, construction paper, colored markers, possibly crayons or paint
Illustrate an island sunset	61	Drawing paper and crayons, markers or paints
Model of machine to pull a fish net out of the water	63	Cardboard tube from a roll of paper towels, a short pencil (for handle), four long pencils (for struts), cheesecloth, string or plants that can be woven into a vine, four or more small plastic fish, rubber bands, shallow pan, modeling clay, water
Shipwrecked song		Optional: accompaniment instrument for the tune "On Top of Old Smoky"
Trojan War play	67	A card table, bedsheets or something else to cover the table, butcher paper, and props such as chairs or tables to make the wall of Troy
How good is a dog's nose?	78	Paper and pencil to write questions and take notes. To find answers to some of the questions, students may need to use CD-ROMs
Research Greek myths	81	Research source materials (dictionaries, encyclopedias, CD-ROMs)
Football display	106	Reference materials on football and poster-making supplies (butcher paper or poster board, markers, crayons, paints, scissors, paste, magazines for pictures)
Animals of Australia	122	Reference materials (Australia books, animal books, encyclopedias, CD-ROMs) and poster-making supplies (butcher paper or poster board, markers, crayons, paints, scissors, paste, magazines for pictures)
Word game	127	Cardstock paper cut into "cards"
Research famous Vikings	143	Biographies of Leif Ericson and Eric the Red
Research George Washington	144	Biography of George Washington
Time line	145	Large butcher paper or poster board (at least 2 feet by 5 feet), markers, crayons, paints, scissors, and other construction materials
Interview		Globe

LESSON INTRODUCED	SENTENCE NUMBER	SENTENCE
4	1	You measure your weight in pounds.
7	2	They waded into the stream to remove tadpoles.
11	3	The fly boasted about escaping from the spider.
14	4	The workers propped up the cage with steel bars.
17	5	Hunters were stationed at opposite ends of the field.
25	6	He motioned to the flight attendant ahead of him.
29	7	The traffic was moving forty miles per hour.
33	8	He is supposed to make a decision in a couple of days.
37	9	Several paths continued for a great distance.
41	10	Boiling water will thaw ice in a few moments.
45	11	They were eager to hear the announcement.
48	12	The lifeboat disappeared in the whirlpool.
52	13	The smoke swirled in enormous billows.
55	14	The occasional foul smell was normal.
58	15	They constructed an enormous machine.
62	16	She survived until she was rescued.
65	17	The soldiers protected their equipment.
68	18	Lawyers with talent normally succeed.
72	19	A dozen typists approached the stairs.
76	20	The job required a consultant.
81	21	The adults huddled around the fire.
87	22	The customer bought a valuable gift.
91	23	They had reasons for interrupting her talk.
95	24	He frequently argued about the championship.
101	25	She commented about the still water.
107	26	Their amazing effort surprised the neighbors.
111	27	Police officers checked the ship's cargo.
115	28	The champions performed perfectly.
118	29	She paid the correct amount.
122	30	Perhaps they will reply in a few days.
127	31	The palace guards spoke different languages.
131	32	His argument convinced them to buy an appliance.
138	33	The army was soundly defeated near the village.

adults *Adults* are grown-ups.

adventure When you have an *adventure,* you do something very exciting.

ahead *Ahead* is another word for *in front.*

Alaska *Alaska* is the largest state.

allow When you *allow* somebody to do something, you permit that person to do it.

although In some sentences, *although* is another word for *but.*

amazing Something that is *amazing* is very hard to believe.

America *America* is a large part of the world.

amount The *amount* of something tells how much there is.

ancient Things that are *ancient* are very, very old.

animal preserve An *animal preserve* is a place that protects animals.

ankles Your *ankles* are the joints right above your feet.

announce When you *announce* something, you let others know about it.

announcement An *announcement* is a message.

apart Things that are not close to each other are far *apart.*

appear When something first comes into sight, it *appears.*

appliances *Appliances* are machines that are used around the house.

approach When you *approach* something, you move toward it.

argue When you *argue* with someone, you tell why you don't agree with what that person says.

argument An *argument* is what you say to make people believe you.

army An *army* is the group of people that goes to war for a country.

arrange When things are *arranged,* the things are in place.

ashamed   When you feel *ashamed,* you feel that you've done something bad.

ashes   The stuff that is left over after something burns up is called *ashes.*

at bat   When a person is *at bat* in a baseball game, that person has a turn at hitting the ball.

attach   Something that is *attached* is connected.

attack   When people *attack,* they do something to start a fight or a battle.

attention   When something catches your *attention,* you know it's there.

Australia   *Australia* is the name of a country.

awful   Something that is *awful* is very bad.

battered   When something is *battered,* it is beaten up.

battle   A *battle* in a war is one of the smaller fights that takes place in the war.

before long   If something happens very soon, it happens *before long.*

behave   The way you *behave* is the way you act.

beyond a doubt   When you know something *beyond a doubt,* you know it for sure.

billows   *Billows* are large clouds or waves that are swelling up.

binoculars   *Binoculars* are powerful glasses that make far-off things look close.

blade   The *blade* is the flat part of a tool that is connected to a handle.

blame   When you say that things went wrong because of somebody else, you *blame* that person.

block   When you *block* in a football game, you push a player from the other team without using your hands to grab the player.

boast   *Boast* is another word for *brag.*

boil   When water *boils,* it makes lots of bubbles and steam. Water boils at 212 degrees.

boiled   Things that are *boiled* are cooked in bubbling hot water.

booms   When a voice *booms,* it's very loud.

bow   (rhymes with *how*) The *bow* is the front of a ship.

bow   (rhymes with *how*) When you *bow,* you bend forward.

broiled   Things that are *broiled* are cooked over an open fire.

buried   When something is *buried,* it has things piled on top of it.

calm   When things are *calm,* they are very quiet and peaceful.

Canada   *Canada* is one of the countries of America.

captain   The *captain* of a ship or plane is the person in charge of the vehicle.

cargo   *Cargo* is what ships carry from one place to another.

catch your breath   When you *catch your breath,* you breathe very hard.

cave   A *cave* is a hole in the ground that is big enough for people or animals to go into.

center   The *center* of something is the middle of the thing.

centimeters   *Centimeters* are used to tell how long things are. There are 100 centimeters in a meter.

certain   *Certain* is another word for *sure.*

championship   A *championship* is a contest between the two best teams.

character   A *character* is a person or animal in a story.

charge   When an animal *charges,* it puts its head down and runs at something as fast as it can go.

Chicago   *Chicago* is a large city near the middle of the United States.

chilled   When you feel cold, you feel *chilled.*

China   *China* is a large country near Japan.

claim   When you *claim* something, you say it's yours.

clomping   A *clomping* sound is the sound a horse makes when it walks on a street.

clue   *Clues* are hints.

coach   A *coach* is the person who gives orders to the players on a team.

coast   The *coast* is where the land meets the ocean.

cock your head   When you *cock your head,* you tilt it.

coconuts   *Coconuts* are fruits with heavy shells.

Columbus   The name of the man who sailed across the

ocean and discovered America is *Columbus.*

comfortable   When something feels *comfortable,* it feels pretty good.

comment   When you *comment* about something, you quickly tell about that thing.

complaint   A *complaint* is a statement that tells what you don't like about something.

completely   *Completely* is another word for totally.

computer   *Computers* are machines that you can use to work problems and play games.

Concord   *Concord* is the name of one of the first towns in the United States.

confusion   When things are very strange and mixed up, we say things are thrown into *confusion.*

constantly   Things that go on *constantly* go on all the time.

construct   When you *construct* something, you *build* it.

consultant   A *consultant* is a person who is hired for a special job.

contest   Any game or event that has winners and losers is a *contest.*

continue   If something *continues,* it keeps on going.

convince   When you *convince* people, you make them believe something.

copilot   A *copilot* is the person who works with the pilot in flying the plane.

correct   *Correct* is another word for *right.*

cottonwood   *Cottonwood* trees are large trees.

count on   When you can be sure of something, you can *count on* that thing.

couple   A *couple* of things is two things.

crate   A *crate* is a wooden box that is used to ship things.

creek   A *creek* is a small stream.

crouch   When you *crouch,* you bend close to the ground.

current   *Currents* are places where water is moving.

customer   A person who buys things at a store is a *customer* of that store.

damage   If you do *damage* to something, you break part of it or ruin it.

danger   When you're in a place where you could get hurt, you're in *danger* of getting hurt.

dates   *Dates* are small sweet fruits that grow on some palm trees.

daydream   When you *daydream,* you think of nice things that you would like to happen.

deaf   People who are *deaf* cannot hear anything.

decision   When you make a *decision* to do something, you make up your mind to do it.

defeat   *Defeated* is another word for *beaten.*

degrees   You measure temperature in *degrees.*

demand   When you *demand* an answer, you insist on it.

Denver   *Denver* is a large city about halfway between Chicago and San Francisco.

describe   When you *describe* something, you tell how it looks or how it works.

destroy   If you ruin something so it can't be fixed, you *destroy* that thing.

direct   Things that are *direct* are straight and simple.

disappear   When something *disappears,* you can't see it anymore.

discover   The person who is the first to find something is the person who *discovers* that thing.

distance   The farther apart things are, the bigger the *distance* between them.

double   *Double* means *two times as much.*

dozen   *Dozen* is another word for *twelve.*

drifts   When something *drifts, winds or currents make it move slowly.*

dull   Things that are boring are *dull.*

during   If something happens *during* the night, it happens while the night is going on.

eager   When you're *eager* for something, you are really looking forward to it.

earlier   Something that happens *earlier* happens before another thing.

earplugs   *Earplugs* are rubber things that you stick in your ears. It is hard to hear when you are wearing earplugs.

earth   *Earth* is another name for our world.

earth   *Earth* is another word for *dirt.*

earthquake   When an *earthquake* takes place, the ground moves and shakes and splits open.

echo   When you hear an *echo,* you hear a sound that is repeated.

effort   Something that takes a lot of strength takes a lot of *effort.*

Egypt   *Egypt* is the name of a country.

electric   Things that are *electric* run on electricity, not on fuel.

electricity   *Electricity* is the power you get when you plug things into wall outlets.

encyclopedia   An *encyclopedia* is a large set of books that gives information about anything you can name.

engine   The *engine* of a vehicle is the part that makes the vehicle run.

England   *England* is a country that is almost 4 thousand miles from the United States.

English   *English* is the name of the language that people speak in England and the United States.

enormous   *Enormous* means *very, very large.*

eohippus   *Eohippus* is the first kind of horse that lived on Earth.

equipment   Large machines and tools are called *equipment.*

escape   When you *escape* from something, you get away from it.

examine   When you *examine* something, you look at it closely.

except   *Except* is another word for *but* in some sentences.

excitement   When you are worked up and have trouble sitting still, you feel *excitement.*

exit   When you *exit* a place, you leave the place.

expensive   Things that cost a lot of money are *expensive.*

explain   When you *explain* something, you give information about that thing.

expression　The *expression* on your face shows what you're feeling.

facts　Sentences that give you information are *facts.*

fades　When something *fades,* it slowly disappears.

fail　The opposite of succeed is *fail.*

faint　When you *faint,* you pass out.

famous　If something is *famous,* it is *well-known.*

fancy　If an office is *fancy,* it is not plain.

fear　If you *fear* something, you are afraid of it.

field goal　A *field goal* is a score in football that is made by kicking the ball.

figure out　When you *figure out* something, you learn it.

finally　*Finally* means *at last.*

finest　Something that is the *finest* is the most expensive or the best.

fire dies down　When a *fire dies down,* it doesn't go out.

fired　When you are *fired* from a job, you are told you can't work at that job anymore.

first base　*First base* is the first base you run to after you hit the ball in a game of baseball.

flight attendant　A *flight attendant* is somebody who works on a plane and takes care of passengers.

force　A *force* is a *push.*

forever　If something lasts *forever,* it never never ends.

foul　*Foul* is another word for *bad.*

frequently　*Frequently* is another word for *often.*

frisky　*Frisky* means *playful* or *full of energy.*

fronds　*Fronds* are the branches of palm trees.

frost　*Frost* is frozen water that forms on grass during cold nights.

fuel　*Fuel* is what engines burn when they run.

gain　When a ball carrier goes the right way in football, he makes a *gain.* When he gets tackled before he can make a gain, he makes a loss.

galley　The *galley* is the kitchen on a plane or ship.

garden　A *garden* is a place where you grow flowers or vegetables.

gift　A *gift* is another way of saying a *present.*

globe   A small model of Earth is called a *globe.*

glows   When something *glows,* it gives off light.

go out for a team   When you *go out for a team,* you show the coach how good you are.

grain   *Grain* is the seed of grass or cereal plants.

gram   A *gram* is a very small unit of weight.

graph   A *graph* is a kind of a picture that has lines or parts that show different amounts.

great   *Great* is another word for *wonderful.*

Greece   *Greece* is the name of a country.

groceries   The food that you buy at the supermarket or grocery store is called *groceries.*

grove   A *grove* of trees is a small group of trees.

guard   A *guard* is a person whose job is to protect something.

gust   A *gust* of wind is a sudden wind that blows for a very short time.

half   If you cut something in *half,* you get two pieces that are the same size. Each piece is half.

half-aware   When you are *half-aware* of something, you are not paying much attention to it.

hallelujah   People who say *"Hallelujah"* are feeling great joy.

harm   *Harm* is another word for *hurt.*

hay   *Hay* is dried grass that horses and cows eat.

heat   When things feel hot, they give off *heat.*

herd   A *herd* of animals is a group of animals that run together.

hoist   When you *hoist* something, you lift it up.

holler   Another word for *holler* is *yell.*

hollow   Something that is *hollow* is not solid.

home run   When a baseball player hits a *home run,* the player hits the ball so far that nobody can get it before the player runs around all four bases.

homonym   A *homonym* is a word that sounds the same as another word.

honest   Here's another way of saying I'm telling the truth: *honest.*

hooves　*Hooves* are the kind of feet that deer and horses and cows have. *Hoof* tells about one foot. *Hooves* tells about more than one foot.

huddle　When people crowd close together, they *huddle.*

human　A *human* is a person.

humans　*Humans* are people.

illegal　Things that are *illegal* are against the law.

imagining　*Imagining* is a kind of thinking.

imitate　When you *imitate* somebody, you do exactly what that person does.

important　If something is *important,* you should pay attention to it.

impression　When you have an *impression* about something, you have an idea about that thing.

in fact　Here's another way of saying that something is true: *in fact.*

India　*India* is a large country on the other side of the world.

insect　An *insect* is a bug that has six legs.

insist　When you keep telling that you want something, you *insist* on that thing.

interrupt　When you *interrupt* somebody, you start talking before the other person finishes.

investigate　When you *investigate* something, you try to learn the facts about that thing.

involved　People who take part in a game are *involved* in the game.

Italy　*Italy* is a country near Greece.

Japan　*Japan* is a country that is 5 thousand miles from the United States.

jewels　*Jewels* are valuable stones.

juggle　When you *juggle* objects, you keep tossing the objects in the air and you make sure that at least two objects are always in the air at the same time.

jungle　A *jungle* is a forest that is always warm and wet.

Kennedy Airport　*Kennedy Airport* is a large airport in New York City.

koala   A *koala* is an animal that looks like a teddy bear and lives in Australia.

lad   A *lad* is a young man.

Lake Michigan   *Lake Michigan* is one of the five Great Lakes.

language   A *language* is the words that people in a country use to say things.

lawn   *Lawn* is the name for grass that is well-kept and mowed.

lawyer   *Lawyers* are people who help us when we have questions about the law.

lean   Something that *leans* does not stand straight up and down.

ledge   A *ledge* is a narrow step that is on cliffs or mountains.

let somebody down   When you *let somebody down,* that person thinks you will help and you don't help.

lifeboats   *Lifeboats* are emergency boats that are on large ships.

lighter   *Lighter* is the opposite of *heavier.*

lookout   A *lookout* is a person who looks in all directions to see if trouble is near.

loss   When a ball carrier goes the right way in football, he makes a gain. When he gets tackled before he can make a gain, he makes a *loss.*

lowered   When something is *lowered,* it is moved down.

machine   A *machine* is something that is made to help people do work.

magnet   A *magnet* is something that hangs on to things made of steel or iron.

magnetic   Things that are *magnetic* stick to a magnet.

make sense   When things don't *make sense* to you, they are not at all clear to you.

make-believe   *Make-believe* is another word for *pretend.*

manage   When you have to work hard to do something, you *manage* to do it.

mean   When you do what you *mean* to do, you do what you plan to do.

measure   When you *measure* something, you find out how long it is or how hot it is or how heavy it is or how tall it is.

mention   When you tell just a little bit about something, you *mention* that thing.

Mexico   *Mexico* is one of the countries of America.

microphone   A *microphone* is a tool that picks up sounds.

million   A *million* is a very, very large number.

million   A *million* is one thousand thousand.

modern   *Modern* is the opposite of *old-fashioned.*

moist   Things that are *moist* are slightly wet, not dripping wet.

moments   A few *moments* is not very many seconds.

motion   When you *motion* to another person, you use your hands or body to show the person what to do.

mumble   When you *mumble,* you talk to yourself so others can't understand everything you say.

mummy   One kind of *mummy* is a dead person all wrapped up in strips of cloth.

muscle   *Muscles* are the meaty parts of your body that make your body move.

myna   A *myna* is a bird.

neighbors   *Neighbors* are people who live near you or sit near you.

New York City   *New York City* is the name of one of the largest cities in the world.

normal   *Normal* is another word for *usual.*

normally   *Normally* is another word for *usually.*

object   When you argue that something is wrong, you *object* to that thing.

occasional   *Occasional* means *once in a while.*

ocean   An *ocean* is a very large body of salt water.

offer   When you *offer* something, you give someone a chance to take it.

Ohio   *Ohio* is a state between Chicago and New York.

open field   An *open field* is a place with just grass and no trees.

opposite   Hot is the *opposite* of cold.

outcome   The *outcome* of an event is the way things turn out.

Pacific Ocean   The *Pacific Ocean* is the ocean that borders the west coast of the United States.

packed   When things are squeezed into a small space, they are *packed.*

palace   A king and queen live in a *palace.* A *palace* is a very large and fancy place.

panel   A flat part that's shaped like a rectangle is called a *panel.*

passenger   A *passenger* is someone who rides in a vehicle.

peacock   A *peacock* is a very large bird with beautiful feathers.

peek   When you sneak a quick look at something, you *peek.*

peel   Another name for the skin of an orange is the *peel* of an orange.

per   *Per* means *each.*

perfect   Something that is *perfect* has everything just the way it should be.

perfectly   If you do something *perfectly,* you don't make any mistakes.

perform   When you *perform,* you put on a show.

perhaps   *Perhaps* is another word for *maybe.*

permit   When you *let* people do something, you *permit* them to do it.

poison   If poison gets inside your body, it will make your body stop working and it may kill you.

police officers   *Police officers* are cops.

poster   A *poster* is a large picture that tells about something.

pouch   A *pouch* is a small bag that holds things.

pounds   *Pounds* are a unit used to measure weight.

practice   Things that you *practice* are things that you do again and again.

preserve   When you *preserve* something, you save it or protect it.

president   The *president* of a country is the person who has the most power to run that country.

pretend   When you *pretend* to do something, you makebelieve.

probably   If something will *probably* happen, you are pretty sure it will happen.

professional football league
A professional football league is a group of teams that play football.

project   A *project* is a large job.

prop up   When you *prop up* something, you support the thing so it will stay in place.

protect   When you *protect* something, you make sure that nothing can hurt it.

prove   When you *prove* something, you show that it is true.

puzzled   Another word for *confused* is *puzzled.*

pyramid   A *pyramid* is a type of building found in Egypt.

queen   Usually, a *queen* is the wife of a king.

raft   A *raft* is a flat boat.

ramp   A *ramp* is a walkway that goes uphill.

raw   Food that is not cooked is *raw.*

realize   When you *realize* something, you suddenly understand if for the first time.

reason   When you tell why you do something, you give a *reason* for doing that thing.

receive   When somebody gives you something, you *receive* it.

recognize   When you *recognize* something that you see or feel, you know what it is.

record   Somebody who sets a *record* does something better than anybody has done before.

referee   A *referee* is a person who makes decisions about how a game is played.

refund   When your money is *refunded,* it is returned.

relatives   Your *relatives* are people in your family.

remain   *Remain* is another word for *stay.*

remove   When you *remove* something, you get rid of it or take it away.

reply   *Reply* is another word for *answer.*

report   When you give a *report,* you give the facts.

required   Things that are *required* are needed.

rescue   Somebody who is *rescued* is *saved* from some kind of danger.

respond   When you *respond* to someone, you answer that person.

rich   If you have lots and lots of money, you are *rich.*

rip-off   A *rip-off* is a bad deal.

rise   *Rise* is another word for *moves up.*

roadside   A *roadside* business is a business that is alongside the road.

ruin   When you *ruin* something, you destroy it or do something to it so it won't work.

rule   A *rule* tells you what to do.

ruler   A *ruler* is a tool that you use to measure inches or centimeters.

runway   A *runway* is like a large road that airplanes use when they take off.

rushing   *Rushing* is another word for *moving fast.*

Russia   *Russia* is the name of a very large country.

salesperson   A person who sells things is a *salesperson.*

San Francisco   *San Francisco* is a city on the west coast of the United States.

scales   The skin of fish is covered with *scales.*

scar   A *scar* is a mark left from a bad cut or burn.

screech   A *screech* is a high, sharp sound.

scold   When your mother *scolds* you, she lets you know what you did wrong.

seasons   Each year has four *seasons:* spring, summer, fall, winter.

sense   Another word for a *feeling* is a *sense.*

service   People who offer a *service* do a special job.

several   *Several* things are more than two things but less than many things.

shabby   Something that is *shabby* is not neat and clean.

shallow   *Shallow* is the opposite of *deep.*

show up   When you go to a place, you *show up* at that place.

skeleton   An animal's *skeleton* is all the bones of the animal's body.

slave   A *slave* is a person who has very few rights.

slight   Something that is *slight* is not very big.

smooth and quiet   When things are *smooth and quiet,* they are very calm.

soldiers   *Soldiers* are men and women in the army.

soundly *Soundly* means *completely* or *really.*

Spain *Spain* is a country that is near Italy.

sped *Sped* is another word for *went fast.*

speedometer A *speedometer* is the dial in a vehicle that shows how fast the vehicle is moving.

spices *Spices* are things that you add to food to give it a special flavor.

spoiled *Spoiled* Students cry and act like babies to make people do things for them.

spy A *spy* is a person who gives important information to the enemy.

stale Food that is *stale* is old and not very good to eat.

stands The *stands* in a ball park are the seats where people sit.

stars The best players are called *stars.*

starve When people have no food to eat for a long time, they *starve.*

stationed When someone is *stationed* in a place, the person is supposed to stay in that place.

steel *Steel* is a very tough metal.

stern The *stern* is the back of a ship.

still Another word for *silent* or *peaceful* is *still.*

strange If something looks *strange,* it does not look like you think it should look.

strength Your *strength* is how strong you are.

stretch When things *stretch* out, they are very wide or very long.

striped If something is *striped,* it has stripes.

strut *Strutting* is a kind of show-off walking.

succeed When you *succeed* at something, you do it the way you planned.

sunken ship A *sunken ship* is a ship at the bottom of the ocean.

support When you *support* something, you hold it up or hold it in place.

supposed to *Supposed to* means *should.*

survive When you *survive,* you manage to stay alive.

swirl When something *swirls,* it spins around as it drifts.

swoop Things that *swoop* move in big curves.

tackle   When you *tackle* players in football, you bring them down so their knees hit the ground.

tadpoles   *Tadpoles* are baby toads or frogs.

takeoff   When an airplane first leaves the ground, it's called the *takeoff.*

talent   People with *talent* are people with special skills.

tame   *Tame* is the opposite of *wild.*

temperature   When you measure the *temperature* of something, you find out how hot it is.

Texas   *Texas* is the second-largest state in the United States.

thaw   *Thaw* means *melt.*

thought   Something that you think about is a *thought.*

thousand   A *thousand* is equal to ten hundreds.

time   When you *time* something, you use a watch to figure out how long it takes.

ton   A *ton* is two thousand pounds.

touchdown   When you score a *touchdown* in football, you take the ball across the goal line.

traffic   All the vehicles that are driving on a street are the *traffic.*

treasure   *Treasures* are things that are worth a lot of money.

triple   *Triple* means *three times as much.*

trumpeting   A *trumpeting* sound is something that sounds like it comes from a musical instrument called a trumpet.

trunk   The *trunk* of a tree is the main part that comes out of the ground.

tumbles   When something *tumbles,* it turns over and over.

Turkey   *Turkey* is a country near Egypt.

tusks   The *tusks* of an animal are huge teeth that stick out of the animal's mouth.

twig   A *twig* is a tiny branch.

typist   *Typists* are people who type things very neatly.

uneasy   When you feel nervous, you feel *uneasy.*

unfair   If rules are not the same for everybody, the rules are *unfair.*

unpleasant   Things that are *unpleasant* are not nice.

usually Things that *usually* happen are things that happen most of the time.

valuable Things that are worth a lot of money are *valuable.*

Viking The *Vikings* were people who lived long ago and sailed to many parts of the world.

village A *village* is a small town.

wade When you *wade,* you walk in water that is not very deep.

war A *war* is a long fight between two countries.

warn When you *warn* people, you let them know that trouble is near.

warts *Warts* are little bumps that some people have on their body. Toads have warts, too.

water strider A *water strider* is an insect that can walk on the top of water.

we'd *We'd* is a contraction for the words *we would* or *we had.*

weak *Weak* means *not strong.*

weather When you tell about the *weather,* you tell about the temperature, the wind, the clouds, and if it is raining or snowing.

weigh When you measure how many grams or pounds something is, you *weigh* it.

weight The *weight* of an object is how heavy that object is.

well A *well* is a deep hole in the ground.

weren't *Weren't* is a contraction for the words *were not.*

whirlpool The water in a *whirlpool* goes around and around as it goes down.

whole *Whole* means all of it—the whole thing.

wise Someone who is *wise* is very smart.

worth Something is *worth* the amount of money people would pay for it.

worthless Something that is *worthless* is not worth anything.

woven Things made of cloth are *woven.*

wrap When you *wrap* a package with paper, you put paper around it.

yard A *yard* tells how long things are. A yard is almost as long as a meter.

age 61	careless 97	dart 17	firewood 126
all 49	caring 97	day 16	fitful 123
almost 17	cart 15	days 27	fitful 115
almost 13	champ 10	deal 21	fitness 111
almost 15	charm 13	deal 84	fitting 111
also 18	cheap 21	decision 87	flame 82
also 17	check 32	deck 31	flame 75
also 13	chop 11	dimly 117	flash 9
also 15	choppy 114	dimly 143	flashing 27
any 114	choppy 127	dining 127	flat 6
any 115	claimed 83	dirty 106	flatly 123
anybody 117	clap 12	dirty 88	flatness 114
anything 117	clapping 130	dirty 28	flatten 116
awful 71	claws 69	doll 49	fold 19
back 26	claws 72	draw 70	food 65
bake 32	clay 18	drawing 72	foods 67
barn 18	clean 77	dream 21	footprint 124
barn 13	clean 73	dripless 137	force 61
bashful 43	clean 81	dripping 143	fork 20
bay 18	clean 24	drive 79	form 19
beach 22	clean 82	dull 28	forms 26
bean 24	clean 29	each 82	found 29
beat 4	cleaner 25	easy 126	freshly 139
beat 24	cleaning 121	eat 3	full 49
bedroom 126	cleanness 43	entering 67	funny 115
bend 2	clearly 71	every 114	furry 116
bending 26	clipped 134	every 115	fuse 79
bike 75	closest 94	everyone 126	game 79
biking 125	cloudy 92	fade 61	game 81
biking 100	coin 62	falling 66	gladly 33
biking 106	coins 83	farm 15	gladly 89
black 31	cold 19	farmer 46	gladly 116
blameless 96	colder 58	farmer 25	gladness 35
body 114	coldest 46	farming 139	glider 99
body 115	coldest 92	fast 5	golden 133
boil 60	coldness 37	fast 7	gripping 116
boil 62	cone 75	fastest 71	gummy 128
boiling 67	count 30	fate 76	handful 36
boldness 33	cowgirl 126	fateful 92	handy 88
bolt 20	crawl 69	fawn 70	happy 28
boy 60	crawling 137	fear 22	harmful 35
boy 63	crawling 71	fearful 48	heat 73
boys 66	crime 4	fearless 66	helped 43
brag 4	crop 5	feast 84	helper 26
brag 9	crop 1	fine 76	helpful 35
brag 1	crop 12	finely 97	helpful 58
bragging 114	crops 120	finely 90	helpful 92
brick 50	cupful 119	fineness 134	helpless 72
broil 63	cupful 112	fineness 96	helplessness 141
camper 37	cupful 115	finest 102	hiding 102
camping 25	cute 82	finest 90	hold 20

LESSON NUMBER	STORY BACKGROUND PASSAGE	MAIN STORY TITLE
1	*Living Things*	The Tiger and the Frog
2	*Make-Believe Animals*	Bob and Don Find Moops
3	*Trees*	Don Washes the White Spot
4	*Apple Trees*	The Little Apple Tree
5	*Forest Fires*	Campers Come into the Forest
6	*Camels and Pigs*	Tina Is Happy
7	*More Facts About Camels*	The Camel and the Pig
8	*Facts About Centimeters*	The Camel and the Pig Trade Parts
9	*Felt-Tipped Pens*	Joe Williams Wants a New Job
11	*Centimeters*	Joe Williams Gets a New Job
12	*Facts About Fleas*	Aunt Fanny's Flea Circus
13	*1) Learning About Time*	
	2) Facts About Flea Circuses	The Fleas Surprise Aunt Fanny
14	*1) Meters*	Aunt Fanny Changes Her Ways
	2) Directions on a Map	
15	*Facts About Toads and Frogs*	Goad the Toad
16	*More Facts About Toads and Frogs*	Goad Uses Her First Trick
17	*1) How Far Apart Things Are*	Food Traps
	2) How Toads Catch Flies	
18	*1) Facts About Moles*	Goad's Four Tricks
	2) The Opposite Direction	
19	*1) Binoculars*	The Brown Family Comes to Catch Goad
	2) How Fast Things Move	
21	*1) Animals and Fire*	The Browns Make Up a Plan
	2) Smoke and Wind	
22	*1) Names That Tell How Fast Things Move*	Goad in the Water
	2) How Air Moves an Object	
23	*Facts About Miles*	A Big Picnic
24	*More Facts About Miles*	Jack and Lisa Have a Race
25	*Telling How Two Things Are Different*	Nancy Wants to Stay Little
26	*Facts About Ants*	A Green Man Visits Nancy
27		Nancy Is Still Tiny
28	*Sugar Shines*	Nancy Finds Something to Eat
29	*1) Water Has a Skin*	Nancy Tries to Get Some Water
	2) Facts About Dew	
31	*More About the Skin That Water Has*	Nancy Gets Some Water
32	*Grams*	Nancy Is Hungry Again
33	*More About Grams*	Nancy Finds Some More Food
34		The Green Man Visits Nancy Again
35	*Sounds That Objects Make*	Nancy Becomes Regular Size
36	*Miles Per Hour*	A Push in the Opposite Direction
37	*More About Pushes in the Opposite Direction*	Herman the Fly
38	*Speedometers*	Herman Goes to Kennedy Airport
39	*Airplane Crew Members*	Herman Ends Up on a Jumbo Jet

LESSON NUMBER	STORY BACKGROUND PASSAGE	MAIN STORY TITLE
41	1) Insects 2) Facts About Speed	Getting Ready for Takeoff
42	Temperature	Herman Takes Off for San Francisco
43	Degrees	Herman Lands in San Francisco
44	Finding the Direction of a Wind	Fly Spray Fills the Air
45	Airplanes and Wind	Rough Air
46	More About the World	Herman Heads to Japan
47	The Eye of a Fly	Herman Tries to Escape
48	1) Facts About Spiders 2) The Size of Some States	The Jumbo Jet Lands in Japan
49		Herman is Cold-Blooded
51	The Air Around The Earth	Herman Flies to Italy
52		Herman's Last Trip
53	1) Facts About Whirlpools 2) Facts About an Ocean Liner 3) Facts About Ocean Water 4) Comparing Things	
54		Linda and Kathy Escape from a Sinking Ship
55	Facts About Islands	Linda and Kathy Find Land
56	Facts About Palm Trees	Alone on an Island
57	Facts About Coconuts	Linda and Kathy Find More Food
58	Facts About Machines	Making Tools
59		Linda and Kathy Construct a Machine
61	Figuring Out the Time of Day	The Girls Have Fish for Dinner
62	Facts About Fevers	Signaling for Help
63	Landing a Ship	The Girls Are Rescued
64	Greece and Troy	Learning About a Time Line
65		The City of Troy
66	When the Story of Troy Took Place	A Great War at Troy
67		The Great Wooden Horse
68		Bertha Has a Great Sense of Smell
69		Maria Gets a Job as an Investigator
71	Oil Wells	Maria Tests Bertha's Talent
72		Maria and Bertha Go to the Oil Refinery
73	Underlined Words	Maria and Bertha Meet Mr. Daniels
74		Bertha Tests Some Water
75		Maria and Bertha Make Up a New Plan
76		Inside a Hot Van
77		The Chief Listens to Bertha
78		Bertha Tests the Water
79	1) Form 50 Special Consultants and Group Leaders 2) Learning About an Achilles Heel	Achilles Heel

LESSON NUMBER	STORY BACKGROUND PASSAGE	MAIN STORY TITLE
81	Chariots	The Greatest Soldier
82		Clues from Thousands of Years Ago
83		Digging Into Piles
84	Fire and Heat	The Cave People Discover Fire
85		Cave Pictures
86		Different Kinds of Horses
87		Horses from Millions of Years Ago
88		How Horses Changed
89	Filling Out a Bank Form	Andrew Dexter Has Daydreams
91	Learning About Checks	Andrew Visits Magnetic Research Company
92		Andrew Is a Changed Person
93	The Strength of Animals	Andrew Gets Fired
94	Learning About Football	Andrew Meets Denny Brock
95	Seconds	The Titans Make Fun of Andrew
96		Andrew Kicks
97	Professional Football Players	Denny Gives Andrew a Job
98		Andrew Plays in His First Game
99		Andrew Meets Smiling Sam
101		Andrew Begins to Change
102		Andrew Plays Harder
103		The Titans Play Harder
104		Andrew Leaves the Team
105		The Championship Game
106		The End of the Game
107	Places You Have Learned About	Looking for Treasures
108	Words That Talk	Hohoboho
109	Liz Takes a Trip	The Words That Sat in the Back Rows
111	Facts About Canada	The Big Change in Hohoboho
112		Run Gets Moved
113	Facts About Australia	Toby the Kangaroo
114	Facts About Kangaroos	A Job for Toby
115	Facts About Peacocks	The Kangaroo Hunters
116	1) Facts About Minutes	Toby on the Ship
	2) Facts About Ships	
117		The End of the Trip
118	More Facts About Canada	The Ship Arrives in Canada
119	Facts About a Circus	Toby's New Job
121	Facts About Boxing	Toby Leaves the Circus
122		The Big Fight
123	Homonyms	The Scarred Words in the Word Bank
124	Henry Ouch Takes a Vacation	The Number with the Most Scars
125	A Pilot's Trip	Some Words Stop Fighting
126		Another Change Is Made
127	Contractions	The Last Problem in the Word Bank Is Solved
128	1) Wooden Buildings	
	2) Time Machines	
	3) More About a Time Line	
129		Eric and Tom Find a Time Machine

LESSON NUMBER	STORY BACKGROUND PASSAGE	MAIN STORY TITLE
131	More About Time	The San Francisco Earthquake
132	1) More About Time	Eric and Tom in Egypt
	2) Facts About Egypt	
133	More About Time	Eric and Tom Meet the King of Egypt
134	Inventing	Eric and Tom Meet the King
135		Eric and Tom Leave Egypt
136	A Queen Named Helen	Eric and Tom in Greece
137	Forty Thousand Years Ago	Eric and Tom See Cave People
138	More About Time	Eric and Tom in the City of the Future
139	1) More About Time	Spain in 1492
	2) North America	
141	More About Time	The Dog and the Time Machine
142	Vikings	The Land of the Vikings
143	More About Time	Trying to Get Home
144	Facts About the United States	Concord
145	More About Time	Home

Guide to Reproducible Appendices

Fact Game

2. a. Does dew form in the middle of the day?

   b. Dew forms when the air gets _____ .

   • warmer • cooler • drier

3. If an ant weighed as much as a cow, the ant could carry an object as heavy as _____ .

4. A mile is a little more than _____ feet.

5. Let's say this line ←————→ on the map is 1 mile long and this line ←——————————→ is 2 miles long.

   a. Say the letter of a line on the map that is 2 miles long.

   b. How far is it from the field to the lake?

   c. How far is it from the park to the forest?

6. What part of the world is shown on the map?

7. One line on the map is 13 hundred miles long.

    The other line is 25 hundred miles long.

    a. How far is it from J to M?

    b. How far is it from K to P?

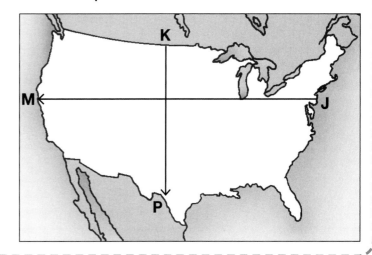

8. Say the part of each name below that tells about time.

    a. inches per week   b. miles per minute   c. meters per year

9. Say the part of each name above that tells about length.

10. a. Which arrow shows the way the air will leave the balloon?

    b. Which arrow shows the way the balloon will move?

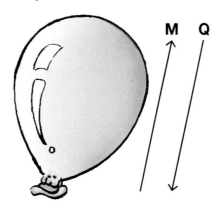

11. The drops of water you can see on grass early in the morning are called _____ .

12. If a grain of sugar were very big, it would look like a box made of _____ .

Fact Game

2. Say the letter of every hair that is being pushed down.

3. Say the letter of every hair that is being pulled up.

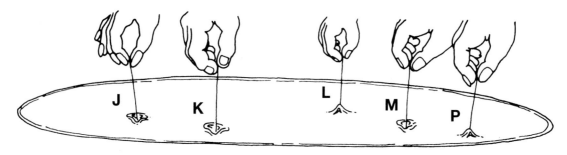

4. When we weigh very small things, the unit we use is _____ .

5. a. How fast is truck A going?

   b. How fast is truck B going?

   c. Which truck is going faster?

   A   **B**

   40   60

6. How far is it from New York City to San Francisco?

7. Tell **how far** or **how fast** for each item.

   a. The bus went 50 miles.

   b. The bus went 50 miles per hour.

Fact Game

8. Tell the letter of the ruler that will make:

   a. the highest sound

   b. the lowest sound

9. When we talk about miles per hour, we tell how _____ something is moving.

10. When something tries to move in one direction, something else tries to move _____ .

11. Say the letters of the 3 animals that eat more every day than they weigh.

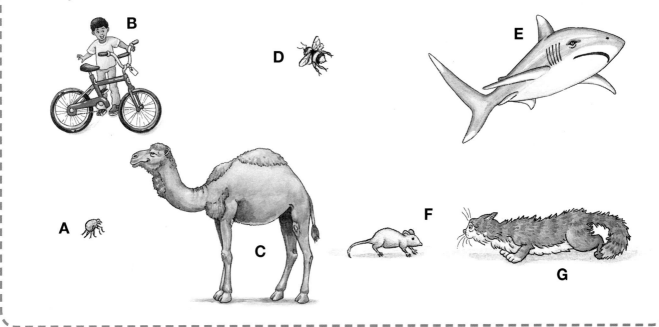

12. If you get smaller, your voice gets _____ .

Fact Game

2. a. Which animal is facing
    into the wind?

    b. Which direction is that animal
    facing?

    c. So what's the name
    of the wind?

3. Tell how fast each object can go.

    a. a fast dog

    b. a jet

    c. a fast man

    - 20 miles per hour
    - 35 miles per hour
    - 200 miles per hour
    - 500 miles per hour

4. Tell the temperature of:

    a. the hottest object

    b. the coldest object

40 degrees   80 degrees   60 degrees

5. Say the names of the cold-blooded animals.

    - ant
    - dog
    - cow
    - bee
    - horse
    - pig
    - flea
    - beetle

6. As you touch places A and B, say the letter. Then tell the name of the place.

7. As you touch places C and D, say the letter. Then tell the name of the place.

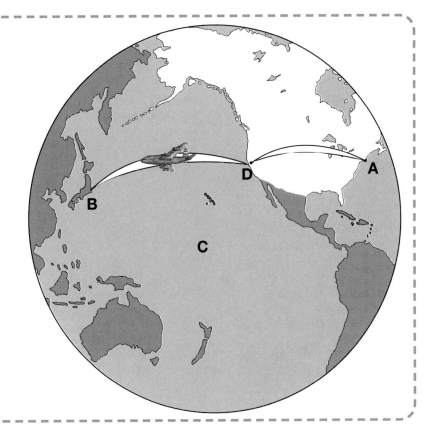

8. How far is it:

   a. from New York City to San Francisco?

   b. from San Francisco to Japan?

9. Answer these questions about the United States.

   a. How many states are there?

   b. What's the biggest state?

10. In which picture is the water

   a. getting hotter?

   b. getting colder?

11. What's the boiling temperature of water?

12. In San Francisco the wind blows from the _____ to the _____ .

Fact Game

2. Say the letter of each island on the map.

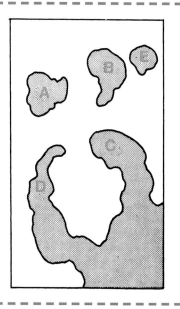

3. Say the letter of the object that will go down the whirlpool:

   a. first

   b. last

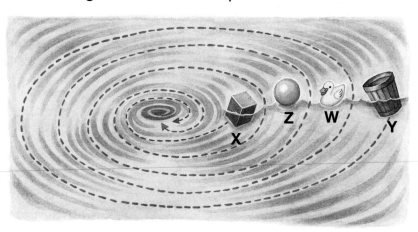

4. a. Which jar is heavier?

   b. Which jar will freeze at 32 degrees?

X — OCEAN WATER   Y — FRESH WATER

Fact Game

5. The arrow by the handle shows which way it turns. Say the letter of the arrow that shows the way:

   a. the log moves

   b. the vine moves

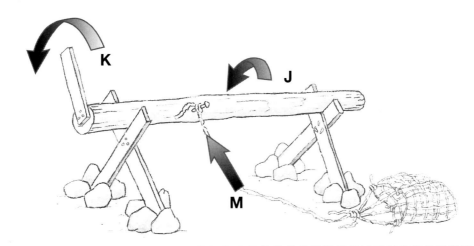

6. As you touch places A and B, say the letter. Then tell the name of the place.

7. As you touch places C and D, say the letter. Then tell the name of the place.

Fact Game

8. Say the letter of the handle that would give you:

   a. the most power

   b. the least power

9. Say the letter of the plane that's in:

   a. the warmest air   b. the coldest air

		5 miles high
	J	4 miles high
	K	3 miles high
L		2 miles high
		1 mile high
	M	

10. Which arrow shows the way:

    a. Linda's hand will move?

    b. the crate will move?

Q ⟶

P ⟵

11. Tell the 3 places that are in the United States.

- Texas   • China

- Italy   • New York City

- Alaska   • Turkey

12. As you touch each letter, say the letter. Then name the part.

Fact Game

2. a. How many ships sailed to Troy?

   b. How long did the war between Troy and Greece go on?

   c. Who won the war?

3. Answer these questions about the war between Troy and Greece.

   a. What did the Greek army build?

   b. What was inside the object?

   c. What did they do after they came out of the object?

4. a. Airplanes are pulled by little trucks. Ships are pulled by _____.

   b. Airplanes unload at gates. Ships unload at _____.

   c. Airplanes land at airports. Ships land at _____.

5. a. When you're healthy, your body temperature is about _____ degrees.

   b. Most fevers don't go over _____ degrees.

6. Tell when

   a. the first airplane was made

   b. the United States became a country

   c. Troy went to war

7. Tell the year

   a. now

   b. 1 hundred years ago

   c. 2 hundred years ago

8. Tell the year

   a. now

   b. 3 hundred years ago

9. As you touch places A, B, and C,
   say the letter. Then tell the name of
   the place.

10. Tell the letter of the sun you see:

   a. at noon

   b. early in the morning

   c. at sunset

11. a. Greece went to war with Troy because of a woman named

   _____.

   b. That woman was important because she was a _____.

   c. She went away with a man from _____.

12. The place that is called Troy is now part of the country of _____.

Fact Game

2. As you touch each letter, say the letter. Then tell the name of the place.

3. a. How long was Troy at war with Greece?

    b. What did the Greek army build?

    c. Who won?

4. Gasoline comes from a liquid called _____ .

5. As you touch each letter, say the letter. Then tell if it shows the **crude oil,** the **pipeline,** or the **refinery.**

Fact Game

6. Which arrow shows the direction the crude oil is moving:

   a. at A?

   b. at B?

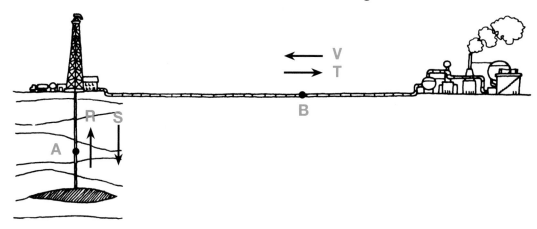

7. As you touch each letter, say the letter. Then tell if it shows **crude oil, salt water,** or **fresh water.**

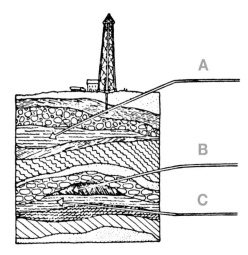

8. Say the sentence using other words for **weakness:** His love of candy was his **weakness.**

9. Name 2 kinds of wells.

Fact Game

10. Which letter shows:

    a. now?

    b. 1 hundred years ago?

    c. 1 thousand years ago?

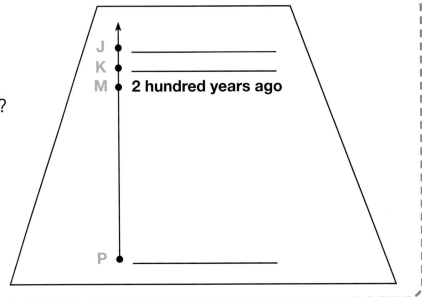

11. Tell when

    a. the United States became a country.

    b. Troy went to war.

12. Tell the year

    a. 1 hundred years ago.

    b. 2 hundred years ago.

Fact Game

2. a. Which army was Achilles in during the war between Troy and Greece?

    b. How long was he in the war?

    c. Who won when he fought against Hector?

3. a. Who was the greatest soldier of Troy?

    b. Achilles rode around the wall of Troy in a _____.

4. a. Name a good place to look for clues about people who lived long ago.

    b. Tell when eohippus lived.

5. As you touch each horse, say the letter. Then name the horse.

A

B

C

6. a. Things closer to the top of the pile went into the pile _____.

    b. Things closer to the bottom of the pile went into the pile

        _____.

Fact Game

7. Which thing went into this pile **earlier?**

   a. W or B

   b. F or H

8. Which thing went into this pile **later?**

   a. W or X

   b. H or B

9. When we dig into the pile, what's the letter of

   a. the first thing we find?

   b. the next thing we find?

   c. the last thing we find?

10. Tell how many third-graders weigh as much as a

    a. draft horse

    b. racehorse

    c. Mongolian horse

11. a. 80 thousand years ago, some people lived in _____ instead of houses.

    b. How does fire like to move, up or down?

12. Which comes first—lightning or thunder?

2. a. Electricity can turn a steel bar into an _____.

    b. Name a place where these magnets are used.

3. a. How long is a football field?

    b. Tell 2 ways that a football team can move the ball down the field.

4. A second is a unit of _____. • length • weight • time • distance

5. a. About how much does a leopard weigh?

    b. About how much weight can a leopard carry?

    • 150 pounds   • 500 pounds   • 100 pounds

6. a. About how much does a chimpanzee weigh?

    b. About how much force can a chimpanzee pull with?

7. As you touch **A** and **B,** say the letter. Then tell how much time has passed on the stopwatch.

8. a. When was this check written?

    b. Who should the bank pay?

> May 20, 1998
>
> **Pay to** _Ted Rose_   ,$15
>
> _Fifteen_ ———————— dollars
>
> _Rod Mack_

9. a. How much should the bank pay?

    b. Whose money should the bank use?

10. Tell the letter of:

   a. the shortest hang-time

   b. the longest hang-time

   A – 6 seconds   C – 2 seconds

   B – 4 seconds   D – 3 seconds

11. As you touch **A** and **B,** say the letter. Then name the part of the uniform.

12. If the hang-time for a kick is 6 seconds, how long does the ball stay in the air?

Fact Game

2. As you touch each horse, say the letter. Then name the horse.

A   B   C

3. a. Things closer to the bottom of the pile went into the pile
_____.

   b. Things closer to the top of the pile went into the pile _____.

4. When we dig into the pile, what's the letter of

   a. the first thing we find?
   b. the next thing we find?
   c. the last thing we find?

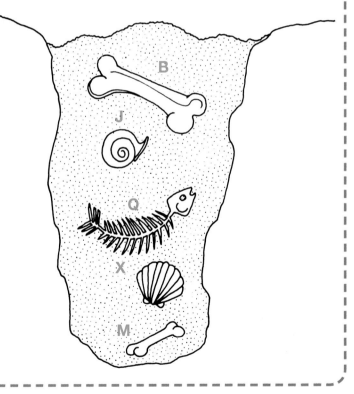

5. Read all the relatives of the word **hop.**

   • hopped   • mopping   • hotter

   • shot   • hopper   • hopping

Fact Game

6. Read all the words in the **walk** family.

- jump
- book
- eats
- walker

- running
- rider
- walks
- runner

- sat
- ran
- walked
- talking

7. Read all the words in the **run** family.

8. As you touch each letter, say the letter. Then tell the name of the place.

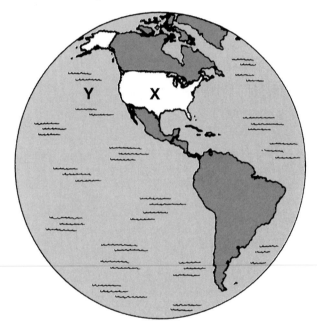

9. As you touch each letter, say the letter. Then tell the name of the place.

10. What happened in place **M** about 3 thousand years ago?

11. Tell the year

    a. the United States became a country.

    b. the first airplane was made.

12. Tell the year

    a. 1 hundred years ago.

    b. 2 hundred years ago.

Fact Game

2. Answer these questions about a kangaroo:

    a. How far can it go in one jump?

    b. How long is it when it's born?

3. a. Where does a baby kangaroo live right after it's born?

    b. How long does it live there?

4. Tell which country:

    a. is just north of the United States

    b. has wild kangaroos

    c. has wild peacocks

5. If you go east from Australia, what ocean do you go through?

6. As you touch A and B, say the letter. Then tell the name of the place.

7. As you touch C, D and E, say the letter. Then tell the name of the place.

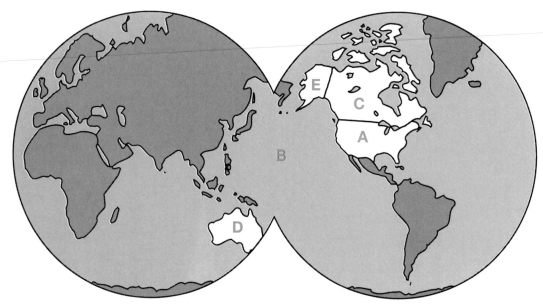

8. How many seconds are in one minute?

9. Answer these questions about Canada and the United States:

   a. Which country is **smaller?**

   b. Which country is **colder?**

   c. Where do **more** people live?

10. The hand on the clock that moves fast went around 5 times. How much time passed?

11. a. What's a group of kangaroos called?

    b. What's a baby kangaroo called?

12. As you touch each letter, say the letter. Then tell the name of the animal.

2. What do we call the mittens that boxers wear when they box?

3. A word that sounds the same as another word is called a _____.

---

4. Which picture shows:

   a. the largest force?

   b. the smallest force?

   H   J   K   M   N

---

5. a. Which city had a great fire that burned down most of the city?

   b. In what year was that fire?

6. Tell the two words that make up:

   a. can't

   b. you've

   c. we're

7. For each word in the box, read the word. Then tell the letter of the word's homonym.

right	A – for
here	B – road
rode	C – write
four	D – hear

Fact Game

8. a. In a large city, what kind of buildings may be made of wood?

   • houses   • stores   • barns   • office buildings

   b. What kind of buildings are not made of wood?

9. Tell what year:

   a. Eric and Tom found the time machine.

   b. Thrig was from.

10. a. A force is a _____.

    b. The greater the force, the harder the _____.

11. Someone in Hohoboho said, "He has a **tear** on his cheek." The word that got the point rhymes with _____.

    • here   • hair

12. What do you do to:

    a. close the door of the time machine?

    b. make the time machine move in time?

Fact Game

2. Tell the 3 years that are in the past.

3. Tell the 3 years that are in the future.

- 1868
- 2100
- 1796
- 2010
- 1996
- 2222

4. Say the 3 names that tell about distance or length.

5. Say the 3 names that tell about time.

6. Say the 3 names that tell about speed.

- inches per minute
- yards
- days
- hours
- meters per week
- feet
- feet per second
- centimeters
- weeks

Fact Game

10. As you touch countries A, B, and C, say the letter. Then tell the name of the country.

11. As you touch countries D and E, say the letter. Then tell the name of the country.

AFRICA

12. Tell the 3 places that are in the United States.

- Texas
- Greece
- Spain
- Canada
- New York
- Concord

7. As you touch dots A, B, and C, say the letter. Then read the event and tell what time each event tells about.

8. As you touch dots D, E, and F, say the letter. Then tell what time each event tells about.

9. As you touch dots G, H, and I, say the letter. Then tell what time each event tells about.

A Eric and Tom were in the city of the future.

B The year Thrig was from

C Now

D You were born.

E Eric and Tom were in San Francisco.

F The United States became a country.

G Greece and Troy went to war.

H Eric and Tom were in Egypt.

I Eric and Tom saw a saber-toothed tiger.

Fact Game Scorecards

Lesson 30

1	2	3	4	5
6	7	8	9	10
11	12	13	14	15
16	17	18	19	20

Lesson 40

1	2	3	4	5
6	7	8	9	10
11	12	13	14	15
16	17	18	19	20

Lesson 50

1	2	3	4	5
6	7	8	9	10
11	12	13	14	15
16	17	18	19	20

Lesson 60

1	2	3	4	5
6	7	8	9	10
11	12	13	14	15
16	17	18	19	20

Lesson 70

1	2	3	4	5
6	7	8	9	10
11	12	13	14	15
16	17	18	19	20

Lesson 80

1	2	3	4	5
6	7	8	9	10
11	12	13	14	15
16	17	18	19	20

Lesson 90

1	2	3	4	5
6	7	8	9	10
11	12	13	14	15
16	17	18	19	20

Lesson 100

1	2	3	4	5
6	7	8	9	10
11	12	13	14	15
16	17	18	19	20

Lesson 110

1	2	3	4	5
6	7	8	9	10
11	12	13	14	15
16	17	18	19	20

Lesson 120

1	2	3	4	5
6	7	8	9	10
11	12	13	14	15
16	17	18	19	20

Lesson 130

1	2	3	4	5
6	7	8	9	10
11	12	13	14	15
16	17	18	19	20

Lesson 140

1	2	3	4	5
6	7	8	9	10
11	12	13	14	15
16	17	18	19	20

Teacher _____   *Reading Mastery Signature Edition*   **Group** _____
                                        Grade 2

Lessons	__1	__2	__3	__4	CO __5	__6	__7	__8	__9	CO/Test __	
Main Story Errors											■
Name	IW	IW	IW	IW	CO	IW	IW	IW	IW	IW	CO	Test

Teacher Ms. Turner

Reading Mastery Signature Edition Grade 2

Group 2

Reading Checkout lessons

Independent Work

Name	4-1 IW	4-2 IW	4-3 IW	4-4 IW	4-5 CO	4-5 IW	4-6 IW	4-7 IW	4-8 IW	4-9 IW	CO/Test 5 CO	CO/Test 5 Test
Main Story Errors	11	12	10	12		(16)	11	10	14	12		
Luis Cepeda	2	1	2	1	P / 0	2	1	0	1	3	P / 0	2
Yoko Higashi	(4)	3	2	2	P / 0	2	3	1	2	2	P / 1	2
Anita Diaz	1	1	1	0	P / 0	2	1	1	0	2	P / 0	0
Denise Barton	1	2	0	1	(F) / 1	1	0	1	0	2	P / 2	(5)
Zachary Gray	1	0	0	1	P / 0	1	2	1	1	1	P / 0	0
Eric Adler	2	1	1	0	P / 1	1	0	1	0	2	P / 1	2

For all categories, circle any non-passing mark.

Main Story Errors Record number of errors group makes during main-story reading.

Independent Work (IW) Record number of errors. Passing criterion: 3 or fewer errors.

Reading Checkouts (CO) Record number of errors in lower part of box. Record **P** or **F** in upper part of box. Passing (P) is 100 (or more) wpm with 2 or fewer errors.

Test Record number of errors. See Test Summary Sheet (Appendix I) for passing criteria.

For more details, see pages 42, 57, 60, and 67 of this guide.

Name	Test 1	Test 2	Test 3	Test 4	Test 5	Test 6	Test 7	Test 8
	1–24	1–22	1–25	1–26	1–33	1–32	1–36	1–19
	1–24	1–22	1–25	1–26	1–33	1–32	1–36	1–19
	1–24	1–22	1–25	1–26	1–33	1–32	1–36	1–19
	1–24	1–22	1–25	1–26	1–33	1–32	1–36	1–19
	1–24	1–22	1–25	1–26	1–33	1–32	1–36	1–19
	1–24	1–22	1–25	1–26	1–33	1–32	1–36	1–19
	1–24	1–22	1–25	1–26	1–33	1–32	1–36	1–19
Passing Criterion	22/24	20/22	22/25	23/26	30/33	29/32	32/36	17/19

APPENDIX I TEST SUMMARY SHEET

Name	Test 9	Test 10	Test 11	Test 12	Test 13	Test 14	End-of-Program Test
	1–30	1–27	1–18	1–32	1–33	1–36	1–30
	1–30	1–27	1–18	1–32	1–33	1–36	1–30
	1–30	1–27	1–18	1–32	1–33	1–36	1–30
	1–30	1–27	1–18	1–32	1–33	1–36	1–30
	1–30	1–27	1–14	1–32	1–33	1–36	1–30
	1–30	1–27	1–14	1–32	1–33	1–36	1–30
	1–30	1–24	1–14	1–30	1–33	1–36	1–30
Passing Criterion	27/30	24/27	16/18	29/32	30/33	32/36	27/30

Reading Mastery Grade 2 Teacher's Guide

50

45

40

35

30

25

20

15

10

100

95

90

85

80

75

70

65

60

55

145
140
135
130
125
120
115
110
105

Grade 2, Letter 1

To the family of _____

This school year your student is enrolled in the *Reading Mastery Signature Edition* program. *Reading Mastery Signature Edition,* Grade 2 will help your student learn the reading skills needed to succeed in school. Your student will learn how to sound out difficult words and read well and quickly. Your student will learn how to remember information that is important and how to use that information to answer questions. And best of all, your student will find that reading is enjoyable.

In *Reading Mastery Signature Edition,* Grade 2, your student will develop the ability to "read to learn." That means your student will be able to read with better understanding in subjects such as science and social studies. In addition, your student will work on important writing and language arts skills.

The best thing you can do this year is to let your student know that the work done in *Reading Mastery Signature Edition,* Grade 2 is very important. Encourage your student to read something at home every day. Remind your student "the more you read, the better reader you will be."

If you have any questions or want more ideas about how to help your student with reading this year, please call me at the school. I'll be happy to talk with you.

Thank you,

_____

Grado 2, Carta 1

Para la familia de _____

     Este año escolar su hijo(a) está inscrito en el programa de *Reading Mastery Signature Edition*. *Reading Mastery Signature Edition*, Grado 2 ayudará a su hijo(a) a aprender las destrezas de lectura necesarias para triunfar en la escuela. Su hijo(a) aprenderá a pronunciar palabras difíciles y a leer mejor y rápido. Aprenderá a recordar información que es importante y cómo usarla para responder a preguntas. Y lo mejor de todo es que su hijo(a) descubrirá que leer es divertido.

     En *Reading Mastery*, Grado 2, su hijo(a) desarrollará la capacidad de "leer para aprender". Esto significa que su hijo(a) será capaz de leer entendiendo mejor las materias como las ciencias y los estudios sociales. Además trabajará en destrezas de escritura y las artes del lenguaje importantes.

     Lo mejor que usted puede hacer este año es dejar que su hijo(a) sepa que el trabajo que hace en *Reading Mastery*, Grado 2, es muy importante. Anímelo(la) a leer algo en casa diariamente. Recuérdele a su hijo(a) que "mientras más lea, un mejor lector será".

     Si tiene alguna pregunta o quiere más ideas acerca de cómo ayudar a su hijo(a) con la lectura este año, por favor llámeme a la escuela. Me encantará hablar con usted.

Gracias,

_____

Grade 2, Letter 2

To the family of _____

   Your student has completed _____ lessons of *Reading Mastery Signature Edition,* Grade 2. Every day your student has worked on skills needed to read better and faster. During this school term, your student has learned how to read hundreds of new words. Every day, your student has read information articles and stories. Your student has learned how to remember and use the information read in the articles and stories. These are important skills that will lead to success next year in school and in all the years to come.

   During this break in the school year, encourage your student to read something every day. As in anything we attempt to learn, reading takes practice and lots of it. Remind your student "the more you read, the better reader you will be." Tell your student you are proud of the progress he or she is making.

   If you have any questions or want more ideas about how to help your student with reading during this break in the school year, please call me at the school. I'll be happy to talk with you.

Thank you,

_____

Grado 2, Carta 2

Para la familia de _____

    Su hijo(a) ha terminado _____ lecciones de *Reading Mastery Signature Edition,* Grado 2. Cada día su hijo(a) ha trabajado en las destrezas necesarias para leer mejor y más rápido. Durante este período escolar su hijo(a) ha aprendido cómo leer cientos de palabras nuevas. Su hijo(a) ha leído artículos informativos e historias diariamente. Ha aprendido cómo recordar y usar la información que leyó en los artículos e historias. Estas son destrezas importantes que conducirán al éxito en el próximo año escolar y en los años venideros.

    Durante este receso del año escolar, anime a su hijo(a) a leer algo diariamente. La lectura requiere mucha práctica al igual que todo lo que intentamos aprender. Recuérdele a su hijo(a) que "mientras más lea, un mejor lector será". Dígale que usted está orgulloso(a) de su progreso.

    Si usted tiene preguntas o quiere más ideas acerca de cómo ayudar a su hijo(a) con la lectura durante este receso del año escolar, por favor llámeme a la escuela. Me encantará hablar con usted.

Gracias,

_____

71

A

1
1. Mr. Daniels
2. recognize
3. elevator
4. medicine
5. guess
6. dozen

2
1. silently
2. watering
3. heater
4. approached
5. fairly

3
1. clues
2. doctors
3. offices
4. drugs
5. typists
6. lawyers

4
1. cock your head
2. equipment
3. motorcycle
4. refinery
5. friendly
6. unfriendly

5
1. explain
2. insist
3. honest
4. crude
5. fifth

6
1. narrow
2. prison
3. polite
4. several
5. pipeline

B

Oil Wells

A well is a deep hole in the ground. The well has pipe in it so the hole stays open.

There are different types of wells.

- Some wells are fresh-water wells. These wells pump fresh water from under the ground.

- Some wells are oil wells. These wells pump crude oil from under the ground.

Picture 1 shows a machine that is drilling a hole for a well.

If the machine keeps drilling, what type of liquid will it reach first?

If the machine keeps drilling past the fresh water, what kind of liquid will it reach next?

If the machine keeps drilling, what will it reach after the oil?

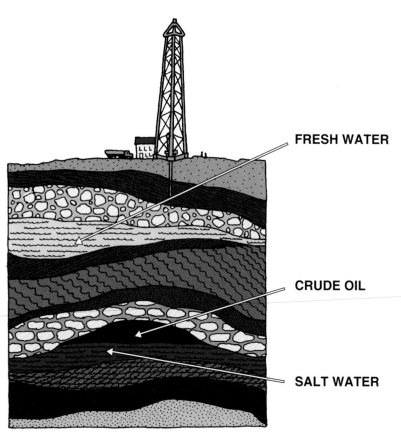

FRESH WATER

CRUDE OIL

SALT WATER

PICTURE 1

If the well is an oil well, it pumps crude oil from the ground. Crude oil is a dark liquid that can be changed to make things like gasoline, motor oil, and plastic.

The crude oil is pumped from the well. Then it goes into a pipeline. The pipeline goes along the ground and carries the crude oil many miles to a refinery.

The refinery is a large place with strange-looking equipment and large tanks for holding oil.

The refinery changes crude oil into gasoline and other things.

PICTURE 2

C Maria Tests Bertha's Talent

Bertha had a plan for helping Maria figure out where the water came from. You probably know what her plan was. Although Bertha didn't know too much about oil wells and refineries, she did know that she could smell the difference between water taken from the creek and water taken from water wells.

Bertha was sitting on Maria's porch. She said, "Maria, it's easy for me to tell if the water comes from the creek or from the well. I'll just smell it."

Maria looked slowly at Bertha and made a face. "What are you talking about?"

Bertha said, "Take me with you and I'll tell you where the water comes from."

Maria made another face. "How will you know where it comes from?"

"I told you. I'll smell it," Bertha said. Then she explained her talent. "I can tell about anything by smelling it. Honest I can."

Maria cocked her head and looked at Bertha. "What is this, a joke?" Maria asked.

Bertha said, "Give me a test. Get glasses of water from different places. I'll tell you where you got each glass of water." At first Maria didn't want to do it. "This is crazy," she kept saying. But Bertha kept insisting on the test. Finally Maria went into her house and came back with three glasses of water. She said, "You ⭐ can't feel them, or you may get some clues about where I got them."

Bertha said, "I don't have to feel them. The one on the left is from your water heater. The middle glass is from a watering can or something like that. That water has been sitting out for a couple of days. The water in the last glass came from a water jug or something in your refrigerator. It's been in the refrigerator for a long time, and it probably doesn't taste very good."

"I don't believe this," Maria said, and she tasted the water from the last glass. She made a face. "Oh, you're right. It's bad."

Suddenly Maria laughed, turned around, and looked at Bertha. She said, "I don't believe this." Then she said, "I don't believe this," three or four more times. "You're amazing. You are amazing. You are the most amazing person I have ever seen."

She kept talking very fast. She told about some of the amazing things that she had seen—a cow with two heads and a building over 3 hundred meters high. Finally, she said, "I once saw a man jump a motorcycle over twenty cars and that was amazing, but you are five times as amazing."

"Can I go with you?" Bertha asked.

"Yes, yes, yes, yes, yes," Maria said. "This will be great."

MORE NEXT TIME

Number your paper from 1 through 19.

Skill Items

Lawyers with talent normally succeed.

1. What word means the opposite of **fail?**
2. What word names people who help us when we have questions about the law?
3. What word means **usually?**
4. What word refers to the special skills a person has?

Review Items

5. You can see drops of water on grass early in the morning. What are those called?

6. Which letter shows the coconut milk?
7. Which letter shows the inner shell?
8. Which letter shows the coconut meat?
9. Which letter shows the outer shell?

10. All machines make it easier for someone to .

11. You would have the most power if you pushed against one of the handles. Which handle is that?

12. Which handle would give you the least amount of power?

13. When people have very high fevers, how do they feel?

14. They may see and hear things that are not .

15. Write the letter that shows a tugboat.

16. Write two letters that show ships.

17. Write two letters that show docks.

18. The place that is called Troy is now part of what country?
    • Greece   • Italy   • Turkey

19. Write the letters of the **4** kinds of weapons that soldiers used when they had battles with Troy.

   a. bows   c. arrows   e. spears   g. planes
   b. swords   d. rockets   f. guns   h. tanks

Name _____

Ⓐ

1. Name two kinds of wells. _____

Write these names on the picture to show where each liquid is: **crude oil, fresh water, salt water.**

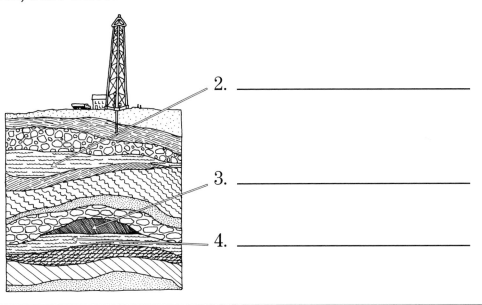

2. _____

3. _____

4. _____

5. Fill in the boxes with the names for the **crude oil, pipeline,** and **refinery.**

6. Draw an arrow at A to show which way the crude oil is moving.

7. Draw an arrow at B to show which way the crude oil is moving.

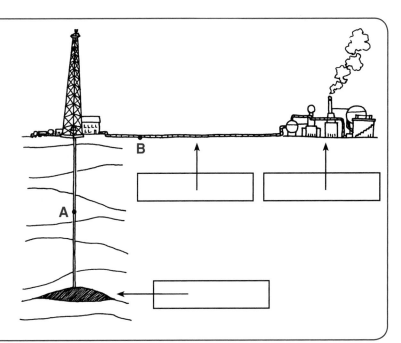

B Story Items

8. Gasoline comes from a liquid called _____.

9. When Bertha first told Maria about her talent, did Maria believe her?

_____

10. How many glasses of water did Maria use to test Bertha's talent?

_____

11. **Underline** the items that tell where the water came from.

- fish bowl   • bath tub   • jug in refrigerator   • sink
- • water heater   • frog pond   • watering can

12. Did Bertha pass Maria's test? _____

13. After the test, did Maria believe what Bertha said about her talent?

_____

14. Bertha will help Maria by telling where ▮▮▮.

- the oil wells are   • the water came from   • the snow was

Review Items

15. The arrow by the handle shows which way it turns. Which arrow

shows the way the log moves? _____

16. Which arrow shows the way the vine moves? _____

GO TO PART D IN YOUR TEXTBOOK.

EXERCISE 1

Vocabulary Review

a. You learned a sentence that tells how long she survived.
- Everybody, say that sentence. Get ready. (Signal.) *She survived until she was rescued.*
- (Repeat until firm.)

b. You learned a sentence that tells what the soldiers did.
- Say that sentence. Get ready. (Signal.) *The soldiers protected their equipment.*
- (Repeat until firm.)

c. Here's the last sentence you learned: Lawyers with talent normally succeed.
- Everybody, say that sentence. Get ready. (Signal.) *Lawyers with talent normally succeed.*
- (Repeat until firm.)

d. Everybody, what do we call people who help us when we have questions about the law? (Signal.) *Lawyers.*
- What's another word for **usually?** (Signal.) *Normally.*
- What word refers to the special skills a person has? (Signal.) *Talent.*
- What word means the opposite of **fail?** (Signal.) *Succeed.*

e. Once more. Say the sentence that tells about lawyers with talent. Get ready. (Signal.) *Lawyers with talent normally succeed.*

EXERCISE 2

Reading Words

Column 1

a. **Find lesson 71 in your textbook.** ✔
- Touch column 1. ✔
- (Teacher reference:)

1. Mr. Daniels	4. medicine
2. recognize	5. guess
3. elevator	6. dozen

b. Number 1 is the name **Mr. Daniels.** What name? (Signal.) *Mr. Daniels.*

c. Word 2 is **recognize.** What word? (Signal.) *Recognize.*

- When you **recognize** something that you see or feel, you know what it is. Here's another way of saying **She knew what the smell was: She recognized the smell.**

d. Your turn. What's another way of saying **She knew what the smell was?** (Signal.) *She recognized the smell.*
- (Repeat step d until firm.)

e. What's another way of saying **She knew who the person was?** (Signal.) *She recognized the person.*

f. Word 3 is **elevator.** What word? (Signal.) *Elevator.*
- Spell **elevator.** Get ready. (Tap for each letter.) *E-L-E-V-A-T-O-R.*

g. Word 4 is **medicine.** What word? (Signal.) *Medicine.*
- Spell **medicine.** Get ready. (Tap for each letter.) *M-E-D-I-C-I-N-E.*

h. Word 5 is **guess.** What word? (Signal.) *Guess.*
- Spell **guess.** Get ready. (Tap for each letter.) *G-U-E-S-S.*

i. Word 6 is **dozen.** What word? (Signal.) *Dozen.*
- Spell **dozen.** Get ready. (Tap for each letter.) *D-O-Z-E-N.*

j. Let's read those words again, the fast way.
- Number 1. What words? (Signal.) *Mr. Daniels.*

k. Word 2. What word? (Signal.) *Recognize.*
- (Repeat for words 3–6.)

l. (Repeat steps j and k until firm.)

Column 2

m. Find column 2. ✔
- (Teacher reference:)

1. silently	4. approached
2. watering	5. fairly
3. heater	

- All these words have endings.

n. Word 1. What word? (Signal.) *Silently.*
- (Repeat for words 2–5.)

o. (Repeat step n until firm.)

Column 3

p. Find column 3. ✔
- (Teacher reference:)

1. clues	4. drugs
2. doctors	5. typists
3. offices	6. lawyers

- All these words end with the letter **S**.

q. Word 1. What word? (Signal.) *Clues.*
- (Repeat for words 2–6.)

r. (Repeat step q until firm.)

Column 4

s. Find column 4. ✔
- (Teacher reference:)

1. cock your head	4. refinery
2. equipment	5. friendly
3. motorcycle	6. unfriendly

t. Number 1. What words? (Signal.) *Cock your head.*
- When you cock your head, you tilt it. Everybody, show me how you cock your head. ✔

u. Word 2. What word? (Signal.) *Equipment.*
- (Repeat for words 3–6.)

v. Let's read those words again.
- Number 1. What words? (Signal.) *Cock your head.*

w. Word 2. What word? (Signal.) *Equipment.*
- (Repeat for words 3–6.)

x. (Repeat steps v and w until firm.)

Column 5

y. Find column 5. ✔
- (Teacher reference:)

1. explain	4. crude
2. insist	5. fifth
3. honest	

z. Word 1. What word? (Signal.) *Explain.*
- When you **explain** something, you **tell about it.** Here's another way of saying **She told about her talent: She explained her talent.**

a. Your turn. What's another way of saying **She told about her talent?** (Signal.) *She explained her talent.*
- (Repeat step a until firm.)

b. What's another way of saying **He told about his plan?** (Signal.) *He explained his plan.*

c. Word 2. What word? (Signal.) *Insist.*
- (Repeat for words 3–5.)

d. Let's read those words again.
- Word 1. What word? (Signal.) *Explain.*
- (Repeat for words 2–5.)

e. (Repeat step d until firm.)

Column 6

f. Find column 6. ✔
- (Teacher reference:)

1. narrow	4. several
2. prison	5. pipeline
3. polite	

g. Word 1. What word? (Signal.) *Narrow.*
- (Repeat for words 2–5.)

h. (Repeat step g until firm.)

Individual Turns

(For columns 1–6: Call on individual students, each to read one to three words per turn.)

EXERCISE 3

Story Background

a. Find part B in your textbook. ✔
- You're going to read the next story about Bertha. First you'll read the information passage. It gives some facts about wells.

b. Everybody, touch the title. ✔
- (Call on a student to read the title.) *[Oil Wells.]*
- Everybody, what's the title? (Signal.) *Oil Wells.* Ⓝ Ⓓ

c. (Call on individual students to read the passage, each student reading two or three sentences at a time. Ask the specified questions as the students read.)

Oil Wells

A well is a deep hole in the ground. The well has pipe in it so the hole stays open.

- Why does the well have a pipe in it? (Call on a student. Idea: *So the hole stays open.*) Ⓝ Ⓓ

There are different types of wells.
- Some wells are fresh-water wells. These wells pump fresh water from under the ground.

- What do fresh-water wells do? (Call on a student. Idea: *Pump fresh water from under the ground*.) (RF/R)

- Some wells are oil wells. These wells pump crude oil from under the ground.

- What do oil wells do? (Call on a student. Idea: *Pump crude oil from under the ground*.) (RF/R)

Picture 1 shows a machine that is drilling a hole for a well.

PICTURE1

- Everybody, touch the underground pipe in picture 1 and show how far down the well is already dug. ✔

If the machine keeps drilling, what type of liquid will it reach first?

- Everybody, touch the liquid it will reach first. ✔
- What kind of liquid is that? (Signal.) *Fresh water*. (VA)

If the machine keeps drilling past the fresh water, what kind of liquid will it reach next?

- Everybody, touch the liquid it will reach next. ✔
- What kind of liquid is that? (Signal.) *Crude oil*. (VA)

If the machine keeps drilling, what will it reach after the oil?

- Everybody, touch the liquid it will reach next. ✔
- What kind of liquid is that? (Signal.) *Salt water*. (VA)
- If you dig a well deep enough, you'll always hit salt water.

If the well is an oil well, it pumps crude oil from the ground. Crude oil is a dark liquid that can be changed to make things like gasoline, motor oil, and plastic.

- What can be made from crude oil? (Call on a student.) *Gasoline, motor oil, plastic*. (RF/R)

The crude oil is pumped from the well. Then it goes into a pipeline.

- Everybody, where does the crude oil go from the well? (Signal.) *Into a pipeline*. (RF/R)

The pipeline goes along the ground and carries the crude oil many miles to a refinery.

- Everybody, where does the pipeline take the crude oil? (Signal.) *To a refinery*. (RF/R)
- Is the refinery usually right next to the well? (Signal.) *No*. (RF/R)

The refinery is a large place with strange-looking equipment and large tanks for holding oil.
The refinery changes crude oil into gasoline and other things.

PICTURE 2

- What does the refinery do? (Call on a student. Idea: *Changes crude oil into gasoline and other things*.) (RF/R)
- Everybody, touch the crude oil underground in picture 2. ✔
- Now follow it up the pipe to the surface of the ground. ✔
- Now follow it in the pipeline to the other end of the pipeline. ✔

- What's the other end? (Signal.) *The refinery.* (VA)
- What does that refinery do to the crude oil? (Call on a student. Idea: *Changes it into gasoline and other things.*) (RF/R)
- The oil company that you're reading about is a refinery.

EXERCISE 4

Story Reading

a. Find part C in your textbook. ✔
- The error limit for this story is 9. Read carefully.

b. Everybody, touch the title. ✔
- (Call on a student to read the title.) *[Maria Tests Bertha's Talent.]*
- What's going to happen in this story? (Call on a student. Idea: *Maria will test Bertha's talent.*) (P)

c. (Call on individual students to read the story, each student reading two or three sentences at a time. Ask questions marked **1**.)

- (**Correct errors:** Tell the word. Direct the student to reread the sentence.)
- (If the group makes more than 9 errors, direct the students to reread the story.)

---

d. (After the group has read the selection making no more than 9 errors, read the story to the students and ask questions marked **2**.)

Maria Tests Bertha's Talent

Bertha had a plan for helping Maria figure out where the water came from. You probably know what her plan was.

1. What do you think it was? (Call on a student. Idea: *Get water from the oil company and have Bertha smell it to see whether it came from the creek or water wells.*) (P)

Although Bertha didn't know too much about oil wells and refineries, she did know that she could smell the difference between water taken from the creek and water taken from water wells.

2. Everybody, where was the company supposed to be taking water from? (Signal.) *Wells.* (APK)

2. Where did Maria think it was coming from? (Signal.) *The creek.* (APK)

Bertha was sitting on Maria's porch. She said, "Maria, it's easy for me to tell if the water comes from the creek or from the well. I'll just smell it."
Maria looked slowly at Bertha and made a face. "What are you talking about?"

1. Everybody, show me the kind of face Maria probably made. ✔

1. What was Maria thinking about Bertha? (Call on a student. Idea: *That she was strange or crazy.*) (DCE)

Bertha said, "Take me with you and I'll tell you where the water comes from."
Maria made another face. "How will you know where it comes from?"
"I told you. I'll smell it," Bertha said. Then she explained her talent.

1. How would she do that? (Call on a student. Idea: *By telling Maria how she used her sense of smell.*) (P)

"I can tell about anything by smelling it. Honest I can."
Maria cocked her head and looked at Bertha.

2. Everybody, show me how you cock your head. ✔ (V)

"What is this, a joke?" Maria asked.
Bertha said, "Give me a test. Get glasses of water from different places. I'll tell you where you got each glass of water." At first Maria didn't want to do it. "This is crazy," she kept saying. But Bertha kept insisting on the test.

2. What would she say to keep insisting on the test? (Call on a student. Idea: *Get glasses of water from different places and I'll tell you where each one came from.*) (DI)

Finally Maria went into her house and came back with three glasses of water. She said, "You can't feel them, or you may get some clues about where I got them."

2. What kind of clues could you get by feeling the water glasses? (Call on a student. Idea: *Clues about temperature*.) (APK)

Bertha said, "I don't have to feel them. The one on the left is from your water heater.

2. What's a water heater? (Call on a student. Idea: *A machine that makes cold water get hot*.) (APK)

The middle glass is from a watering can or something like that.

2. What do you do with a watering can? (Call on a student. Idea: *Water plants and flowers*.) (APK)

That water has been sitting out for a couple of days. The water in the last glass came from a water jug or something in your refrigerator. It's been in the refrigerator for a long time, and it probably doesn't taste very good."

"I don't believe this," Maria said, and she tasted the water from the last glass. She made a face. "Oh, you're right. It's bad."

2. Everybody, show me the kind of face she made when she tasted the water. ✔ (V)

Suddenly Maria laughed, turned around, and looked at Bertha. She said, "I don't believe this." Then she said, "I don't believe this," three or four more times. "You're amazing. You are amazing. You are the most amazing person I have ever seen."

She kept talking very fast. She told about some of the amazing things that she had seen—a cow with two heads and a building over 3 hundred meters high. Finally, she said, "I once saw a man jump a motorcycle over twenty cars and that was amazing, but you are five times as amazing."

2. Maria is really excited. I'll read that part again. Listen to how she talks on and on.

Suddenly Maria laughed, turned around, and looked at Bertha. She said, "I don't believe this." Then she said, "I don't believe this," three or four more times. "You're amazing. You are amazing. You are the most amazing person I have ever seen."

She kept talking very fast. She told about some of the amazing things that she had seen—a cow with two heads and a building over 3 hundred meters high. Finally, she said, "I once saw a man jump a motorcycle over twenty cars and that was amazing, but you are five times as amazing."

"Can I go with you?" Bertha asked. "Yes, yes, yes, yes, yes," Maria said. "This will be great."
MORE NEXT TIME

1. Go back to the beginning of the story. Follow along while I read.
2. What do you think is going to happen? (Call on a student. Idea: *Maria will get Bertha to smell the water the oil company uses;* etc.) (P)

EXERCISE 5

Paired Practice

You're going to read aloud to your partner. Today the **B** members will read first. Then the **A** members will read from the star to the end of the story.
(Observe students and give feedback.)

End-of-Lesson Activities

INDEPENDENT WORK

Now finish your independent work for lesson 71. Raise your hand when you're finished.
(Observe students and give feedback.)

WORKCHECK

a. (Direct students to take out their marking pencils.)
• We're going to check your independent work. Remember, if you got an item wrong, make an **X** next to the item. Don't change any answers.

b. (For each item: Read the item. Call on a student to answer it. If the answer is wrong, say the correct answer. Refer to the Answer Key for the correct answers.)

c. Now use your marking pencil to fix up any items you got wrong. Remember, all mistakes must be fixed up before you hand in your independent work.

SPELLING

(Present Spelling lesson 71 after completing Reading lesson 71. See *Spelling Presentation Book*.)

LESSON **71**

EXERCISE 1

Patterns

a. You're going to write words with endings. Some of the words are spelled with the letters **A-W**. Number your paper from 1 through 5. ✔

b. Word 1 is **fastest**. Who can run the **fastest?** What word? (Signal.) *Fastest.*
 • Write the word **fastest.** ✔

c. Word 2 is **roomful**. We had a **roomful** of flowers. What word? (Signal.) *Roomful.*
 • Write the word **roomful.** ✔

d. Word 3 is **awful**. I felt **awful**. What word? (Signal.) *Awful.*
 • Write the word **awful.** ✔

e. Word 4 is **crawling**. The baby was **crawling** across the floor. What word? (Signal.) *Crawling.*
 • Write the word **crawling.** ✔

f. Word 5 is **clearly**. We could see the ship **clearly**. What word? (Signal.) *Clearly.*
 • Write the word **clearly.** ✔

g. Check your work. Make an **X** next to any word you got wrong.

h. Word 1. Spell **fastest**. Get ready. (Tap for each letter.) *F-A-S-T-E-S-T.*
 • (Repeat for: **2. roomful, 3. awful, 4. crawling, 5. clearly.**)

EXERCISE 2

Phonemic Segmentation

a. Listen: **fast.** Say it. (Signal.) *Fast.*

b. I'll say the sounds in **fast:** **fff . . . aaa . . . sss . . . t.**
 • Say the sounds in **fast.** Get ready. (Tap for each sound.) *fff . . .aaa . . . sss . . . t.*

> **To correct:**
> • (Return to step a.)

c. What's the first sound in **fast?** (Signal.) *fff.*

> **To correct:**
> • (Say the correct sound.)
> • (Return to step a.)

d. Next sound? (Signal.) *aaa.*
e. Next sound? (Signal.) *sss.*
f. Next sound? (Signal.) *t.*

g. Listen: **stop.** Say it. (Signal.) *Stop.*
h. I'll say the sounds in **stop:** **sss . . . t . . . ooo . . . p.**
i. Say the sounds in **stop.** Get ready. (Tap for each sound.) *sss. . . t . . . ooo . . . p.*
j. What is the first sound in **stop?** (Signal.) *sss.*
k. Next sound? (Signal.) *t.*
l. Next sound? (Signal.) *ooo.*
m. Next sound? (Signal.) *p.*
 Yes. Those are the sounds in **stop.**
 • (Repeat steps g–m for **spot [sss . . . p . . . ooo . . . t], clap [c . . . lll . . . aaa . . . p].)**

n. (Call on individual students to say the sounds in: **fast, stop, spot, clap.**)

EXERCISE 3

Spelling Review

a. You're going to spell words.

b. Word 1 is **solid**. Spell **solid**. Get ready. (Signal.) *S-O-L-I-D.*

c. Word 2 is **claw**. Spell **claw**. Get ready. (Signal.) *C-L-A-W.*

d. Word 3 is **youthful**. Spell **youthful**. Get ready. (Signal.) *Y-O-U-T-H-F-U-L.*

e. Word 4 is **drawing**. Spell **drawing**. Get ready. (Signal.) *D-R-A-W-I-N-G.*

f. (Give individual turns on: **1. solid, 2. claw, 3. youthful, 4. drawing.**)

Skills Profile Chart

Student's Name_____ Year _____

Teacher's Name _____

School's Name _____ Phone _____

Student's grade in school: _____

Number of days absent: lessons 1-50 _____   lessons 51-100_____   lessons 101-145 ___

Last lesson completed _____   Date _____

Comments:

	Lessons 1-70	Lessons 71-145
Decoding Activities		
Story Reading		
Comprehension Activities		
Areas of Strength		
Areas of needed improvement		

Recommendations:_____

_____

Conference dates and results: _____

_____

_____

_____

_____

_____

READING ACTIVITIES

CATEGORIES	SKILLS	FIRST APPEARS IN LESSON	DATE MASTERED
DECODING SKILLS: SOUNDS	Read the following sound combinations correctly: ce ou ir oa ar al aw oi ee ea (long) mb ew ea (short)	7 7 7 15 18 18 18 23 25 25 26 38 115	
DECODING SKILLS: WORDS	Read each word without error.	1	
	Repeat each word, spell each word, then read each word without error.	1	
	Read words with the following endings: s es ed ing y tion sion ly er n th 's est ment or able ful	1 1 3 4 17 18 18 29 31 37 37 37 43 53 69 75 122	
	Read a list of irregularly spelled words.	1	
	Read the underlined part of a word and then read the whole word.	3	
	Read parts of compound words and then read the entire word.	6	
	Orally read a list of words without making an error.	1	
	Read syllables of a word, then read the entire word.	3	
	Read words with the following beginning sound(s): sw w	55 108	
	Write homonym(s) for a given word. Identify the correct pronunciation of a homograph.	123 126	
	Write the two words that make up a given contraction.	127	
DECODING SKILLS: SENTENCES AND STORIES	Read part of a textbook selection aloud. Read aloud in pairs.	1 6	
	Read part of a textbook selection silently.	92	
FLUENCY CHECKOUTS	Orally read a specified textbook passage in one minute or less with a minimum of decoding errors.	10–150 every fifth lesson	

COMPREHENSION ACTIVITIES

CATEGORIES	SKILLS	FIRST APPEARS IN LESSON	DATE MASTERED
COMPREHENSION SKILLS: READINESS	Follow directions presented orally by the teacher.	1	
	Respond to tasks based on pictures in the textbook.	6	

Comprehension Activites (continued)

COMPREHENSION SKILLS: VOCABULARY	Explain the meaning of a defined vocabulary word.	4	
	Use a vocabulary word correctly in a sentence.	4	
	Read proper nouns correctly.	11	
	Read "time" words correctly.	12	
	Choose a word that means the same thing as an underlined word or words.	16	
COMPREHENSION SKILLS: LITERAL COMPREHENSION	Memorize facts and rules presented in the textbook. Respond orally to facts and rules. Respond in writing to questions in the textbook about facts and rules. Complete workbook exercises by recalling facts and rules.	1 1 1 1	
	Answer literal questions about a textbook selection. Respond in writing to literal questions in the textbook. Complete workbook exercises by answering literal questions.	1 1 1	
	Answer questions about a textbook selection by recalling details and events. Respond in writing to questions in the textbook about details and events.	1 1	
	Complete workbook exercises by recalling details and events. Answer questions about a textbook selection by identifying literal cause and effect. Complete workbook exercises by identifying literal causes and effects.	1 1 1	
	Follow written directions.	1	
COMPREHENSION SKILLS: INTERPRETIVE COMPREHENSION	Predict the outcome of a textbook story.	1	
	Use a textbook story's title to predict its content.	1	
	Answer questions about a textbook selection by inferring causes and effects. Respond in writing to inferential cause and effect questions in the textbook. Complete workbook exercises by inferring causes and effects.	1 1 1	
	Answer questions about a textbook selection by inferring details and events. Respond in writing to inferential detail and event questions in the textbook. Complete workbook exercises by inferring details and events.	1 1 1	
	Use a deduction to complete workbook activities.	1	
	Put events from a textbook story in the correct order.	117	
COMPREHENSION SKILLS: REASONING	Answer questions about a textbook selection by drawing conclusions.	1	
	Complete workbook exercises by using given rules to predict outcomes.	3	
	Complete exercises by using given rules to classify objects.	1	
	Write the conclusion for a formal written deduction.	1	
	Identify the author's purpose in a passage.	51	
	Play the Fact Game.	10–140 every tenth lesson	
COMPREHENSION SKILLS: CONTENT KNOWLEDGE	Retain and use content concepts	1	

LITERARY SKILLS			
CATEGORIES	**SKILLS**	**FIRST APPEARS IN LESSON**	**DATE MASTERED**
LITERARY SKILLS: CHARACTERS AND SETTING	Answer questions about a textbook story by interpreting a character's feelings.	4	
	Answer questions about a textbook story by interpreting a character's motives.	4	
	Answer questions about a textbook story by inferring a character's point of view.	6	
	Answer questions about a textbook story by pretending to be a story character.	13	
	Describe the setting of a story.	4	

Literary Skills (continued)

LITERARY SKILLS: TYPES OF LITERATURE	Read realistic fiction in the textbook.	41–52, 54–63, 68–78	
	Read fantasy in the textbook.	1	
	Read a non-fiction selection in the textbook.	1	
	Read an information passage in the textbook.	1	
	Distinguish between realism and fantasy.	1	
QUOTATION MARKS	Underline what a character said.	8	

STUDY SKILLS

CATEGORIES	SKILLS	FIRST APPEARS IN LESSON	DATE MASTERED
STUDY SKILLS: USING REFERENCE MATERIAL	Write answers to questions about a textbook story presented in either the textbook or the workbook.	1	
	Read information passages in the textbook.	1	
	Complete skill exercises by identifying and applying standard measurements.	8	
	Use a given map to answer questions about direction, relative size, proximity, labels, and other map-related concepts from a textbook story.	14	
	Answer questions about a given diagram.	16	
	Use a globe to answer questions.	46	
	Interpret a timeline.	64	
	Complete workbook exercises by filling out standard forms.	79	
	Complete workbook exercises by filling out a check correctly.	81	
	Use reference materials to write a report.	143	

SPECIAL PROJECTS

CATEGORIES	SKILLS	FIRST APPEARS IN LESSON	DATE MASTERED
SPECIAL PROJECTS	Complete the following Special Projects:	After lesson:	
	Make a large map.	23	
	Conduct an experiment to show that substances like steel can float on water.	35	
	Make a globe of the earth.	52	
	Produce a picture based on a text description.	61	
	Put on a play about the Trojan War.	67	
	Write questions and take notes about a passage; have a guest speaker.	78	
	Use research material to find information about myths.	81	
	Make a display about football.	106	
	Use reference materials to find information about Australian animals.	122	
	Make a word game using synonyms, opposites, and homonyms.	127	
	Write a report about Leif Ericson or Eric the Red.	143	
	Write a report about George Washington.	144	
	Make a time line.	145	

ACTIVITIES ACROSS THE CURRICULUM

CATEGORIES	SKILLS	FIRST APPEARS IN LESSON	DATE MASTERED
ACTIVITIES ACROSS THE CURRICULUM	Complete an activity in a content area.	51	

Table of Contents

Overview of Transition

Reading Mastery Signature Edition, **Transition** is positioned between Grade 1 Signature Edition and Grade 2 Signature Edition. The Transition provides 35 lessons that serve two possible functions.

1. Transition provides lower performers with additional decoding and comprehension practice. Often, these students have difficulties at the beginning of Grade 2, because the story emphasis changes from learning to read to reading to learn. Students who go through the Transition program receive additional practice with content that helps them at the beginning of *Reading Mastery Signature Edition,* Grade 2.

2. **Transition** provides the opportunity for you to consolidate smaller groups at the beginning of the year. If one group has finished the Grade 1 sequence but another group that is on the same skill level has not completed the Grade 1 sequence, you may put the group that is ahead into the Transition program until the other group completes the Grade 1 program. Then you would be able to combine the two groups to make a larger group.

3. Transition is a good supplemental program. If the daily schedule permits, use the Transition program as a supplemental or reinforcement program during the first part of the year. Students find the stories quite reinforcing.

Skill Requirements

Students who enter the *Reading Mastery Signature Edition,* Transition program should be able to decode words that are presented in *Reading Mastery Signature Edition,* Grade 1.

They should have had practice in handling simple reading comprehension exercises, including responding to written questions about stories. The students should be able to read without sounding out and should be fairly proficient at decoding at the rate of about 60 words per minute. Entering students should know all of the words and possess the sentence analysis skills required to decode and understand the selection presented in Lesson 1. (See **The Bragging Rats,** referenced on page 167.)

The *Reading Mastery Signature Edition,* Transition program builds on these skills. The Transition scope and sequence chart on page 169 outlines the track development of the program.

Program Components

The Transition **Presentation Book** contains three sections:

Section I—Teacher's Guide

Section II—Teacher Presentation Book

Section III—Answer Key

Teacher Materials

- **The Teacher's Guide** section provides explanations of the program and how to teach it. The guide section contains rationale for the various conventions and sequence details. It shows key exercises and explains how to teach the exercises and how to correct mistakes the students are likely to make. The guide contains in-program test information, test remedies, and a list of all reading words introduced in word-reading exercises. This section also contains information for placing students, remediating students, and proceeding through the Transition program.

- **The Teacher Presentation Book** section provides the teacher with exercises for directing reading activities for all 35 lessons. The exercises indicate the teacher wording and the correct student responses for each activity. The exercises also include directions for firming responses so that students remember what they are being taught.

- **The Answer Key** section contains answers for all student-written activities in *Reading Mastery, Signature Edition,* Transition reading lessons.

Student Materials

- **One Textbook** contains vocabulary lists, stories, illustrations, and activities for selections students read for the lessons.

- **One Workbook** contains worksheets for the 35 reading lessons and 4 Mastery Tests. The worksheets present comprehension and skill items to test and reinforce what students are learning in the lessons.

Scope and Content

Reading Mastery Signature Edition, Transition provides students with 35 reading lessons. The reading lessons help them develop reading fluency, accuracy, and comprehension skills.

Students who appropriately begin Transition have completed *Reading Mastery Signature Edition* Grade 1. On page 167 is the first selection of *Reading Mastery, Signature Edition,* Transition. Entering students should know all the words and possess the sentence analysis skills required to accurately decode and understand this selection.

The Transition reading program helps students continue to build on these entry reading skills, following the same cycle of skill development used in the earlier levels of the program (from sounds to words to stories).

Each cycle begins with new rules about letter sounds or letter combinations, such as the rule that the letters **ou** usually make the sound heard in **our.**

After the introduction of a new sound, students learn about words that have the new sound. First, students listen to some words that have the new sound. For example, they identify the sound **ou** in words, such as **our, pounce,** and **found.** Next, students decode words that have the new sound. Finally, after students have practiced reading words in isolation for a couple of lessons, the new word type (words with the new sound) appears in stories students read.

Once a word or word type has been introduced in this manner, it continues to appear in stories and independent work so that students develop skills for processing all the words that are taught in the program (not simply the most recently introduced words).

At the end of *Reading Mastery Signature Edition,* Transition, students are able to read stories with an expanded vocabulary at a rate of 90 words per minute.

Story Reading

Story reading is part of every regular lesson. The main goals of story reading are to (1) build decoding skills and (2) promote different strategies for reading for meaning. Students read 34 stories during the group story-reading part of the lessons. For lessons 1–35, Students read from their Textbook. The students respond to a wide range of oral comprehension questions presented by the teacher. In addition, they independently read dozens of comprehension passages during their independent-workbook-practice time.

Grouping

Students should be grouped homogeneously (high, middle, low) with no more than three groups in the classroom. Ideally, a group would not have more than 12 students in it. No group should have more than 15 students.

How to Set Up the Group

1. Seat the students in a semicircle in front of you. Sit so that you can observe every student in the group as well as the students who are engaged in independent work. Students in the group should sit on chairs, not at desks.

2. Place the lowest performers directly in front of you, in the first row if there is more than one row. Seat the highest performers on the ends of the first row or in the second row. You will naturally look most frequently at the students seated directly in front of you. Teach until every student is firm in his or her response. If you are constantly looking at the lowest-performing students, you will know when their responses are firm. When the lowest-performing students' responses are firm, the responses of the rest of the group will be firm.

Group Performance

Students who are appropriately placed in *Reading Mastery Signature Edition,*

Transition should usually complete a lesson a day. However, students should perform at a high level of mastery and should not be overwhelmed with the material they are expected to read.

You may find that with some lessons it takes more than one period to firm all student's responses. When the choice is between firming all the student's responses and completing the lesson, choose the firming. The best procedure is to *firm the students' responses when new skills are first introduced.*

If you find that students typically take longer than 30 minutes to complete the main part of lessons, there is a problem. Either the group is not homogeneous and the students should be regrouped, or there are problems with the way you are presenting the material.

In-Program Mastery Tests

Mastery Tests 1–4 test words in isolation and in story reading. Each student is tested individually on rate and accuracy.

The mastery tests give you feedback on the effectiveness of your teaching, serve as a backup for your daily evaluation of the student's performance, provide information for transitioning the students into Grade 2, and provide you with a basis for giving grades. (See **Mastery Test 1 and an explanation of it** on page 176.)

Program Skill Structure
Scope and Sequence

The Scope and Sequence chart shows the following major activities students engage in during most lessons.

1. Reading words and sounds lists

2. Story reading

3. Comprehension

4. Workbook activities

- Students learn sounds for letter combinations.

- Students orally read a story selection.

- Students orally answer comprehension questions about details of the story they read.

- Students do independent work, which often consists of reading a passage and answering questions about the passage, answering written questions about the story and applying word skills and character knowledge to do a variety of matching and extension activities.

Scope and Sequence

Lessons (1–35)	
Word Attack	
Sounds	Letter Combinations 3–35 Reading Words the Fast Way 1–35 Underlined Word Parts 2–35 Spell-First Exercises 1–35 Rhyming Words 3–35
Stories	
Story Reading	Reading Stories (Oral) 1–35 Reading Comprehension 1–35
Workbook Activities	
Independent Work	Story Extensions 1–35 Story Items 1–34 Writing Words for Pictures/Missing Words and Pictures 6–35 Character Matching Game 1–35 Description Matching Game 3–35 Cross-Out and Circle Game 13–30 Directions Game 2–35 Passage Reading 1–35
Mastery Tests	
Words and Story Reading	After Lesson: 7, 16, 25, 35

Lesson	Combination	Pronounced	As in
5	aw	awe	paw
5	gh	silent	high
5	ge	j	message
5	ce	sss	cent, ice
5	ch	ch	chew
5	qu	koo	quick
5	ou	ow, ou	pounce
7	oi	oy	boil
7	ea	ēēē	teased
9	sh	shshsh	push
9	th	ththth	south
12	dge	j	pledge
12	ai	āāā	tail
13	ew	oooo	chew
13	ar	ar	barge
14	oy	oy	boy
15	or	or	short
29	tion	shun	action
30	oo	oooo	noon
34	sion	shun	mansion
34	shion	shun	fashion

Sounds

The sounds track appears in most lessons, beginning in lesson 5 and continuing through lesson 34. If the lesson has sound-identification exercises, they are the first exercises in the lesson. The table above shows the combinations for lessons 5–34.

Here's an exercise from lesson 5 that presents combinations.

EXERCISE 1

SOUNDS

a. Open your textbook to lesson 5. Find the celery. ✔
- (Teacher reference:)

   aw   gh   ge   ce   ch   qu   ou

- You'll spell each combination, then tell me the sound it makes.
b. Spell the first combination. Get ready. (Tap 2 times.) *A-W.*
   The sound for that combination is **awe.**
- What's the sound? (Signal.) *awe.*
c. Spell the next combination. Get ready. (Tap 2 times.) *G-H.*
   That combination has no sound at all.
- What's the sound? (Signal.) *(No response.)*
   G-H doesn't make a sound.
d. Spell the next combination. Get ready. (Tap 2 times.) *G-E.*
   The sound for that combination is **j.**
- What's the sound? (Signal.) *j.*
e. Spell the next combination. Get ready. (Tap 2 times.) *C-E.*
   The sound for that combination is **sss.**
- What's the sound? (Signal.) *sss.*

f. Spell the next combination. Get ready. (Tap 2 times.) *C-H.*
   • What's the sound? (Signal.) *ch.*
g. Spell the next combination. Get ready. (Tap 2 times.) *Q-U.*
   The sound for that combination is **koo.**
   • What's the sound? (Signal.) *koo.*
h. Spell the last combination. Get ready. (Tap 2 times.) *O-U.*
   • What's the sound? (Signal.) *ow.*

Word Reading

The word-reading-track is similar to *Reading Mastery Signature Edition,* Grade 1. Word-reading exercises appear in every regular lesson (1–34). If no sound-identification exercises are in the lesson, word reading is the first activity. If the lesson has sound identification, word reading follows it.

The work with words usually involves three to five lists. Students read lists twice. They use different strategies to decode the words in these lists on the first reading. They always read the list the fast way on the second reading.

1. For some lists, the students simply identify the words. (See Exercise 4, Sample Lesson 6, page 179.)

2. Another type of list shows part of each word underlined. The students usually identify the underlined part, then the whole word (the words on the Lesson 3 map). Some words with more than one syllable have a familiar part. These words sometimes go into a list that has part of each word underlined. The students read the familiar part first, then the whole word. (See Exercise 1, Sample Lesson 6, page 178.)

3. In another kind of list, the words are spelled, then read (the words on the Lesson 3 board and desk). Sometimes you do the spelling; sometimes the students do. (See Exercises 2, 3, and 6, Sample Lesson 6, pages 178–180.)

4. Another type of list presents rhyming words (the words on the Lesson 3 flags). Sometimes there are pairs of rhyming words; sometimes all the words in a list rhyme. The first word may be familiar. Students read that word. Then they read the word that rhymes, using the information that the words rhyme to pronounce the new word. (See Exercise 5, Sample Lesson 6, page 179.)

5. Some words cannot be easily sounded out. These words go into lists that students read the fast way or lists in which the words are spelled. (Lesson 3 words below the desk.) (See also Exercise 4, Sample Lesson 6, page 179.)

Students read familiar words the fast way. Also, new words that are irregular but not easily confused with other words may initially appear in a list that students read the fast way. (See **Word-Attack Exercises** in sample lesson 6, pages 178–180.)

Reading Mastery Grade 2 Teacher's Guide   **171**

Individual Turns

After students have completed the sounds and word-reading exercises, you present individual turns. These turns are designed to give you information about how well students have learned the material you presented. (See Individual Turns, Sample Lesson 6, page 180.)

Story Reading

Story reading immediately follows the word-attack and individual-turns portion of the lessons. The procedure involves two readings of the story. The first reading focuses on decoding. During this reading, you usually do not present comprehension questions or refer to the story illustrations. All lessons have an error limit. The goal is for the students to read the story without exceeding the error limit.

During the second reading, the focus is on the content of the story. You ask specified comprehension questions and refer the students to the story illustrations.

(See Story Reading, Sample Lesson 6, page 180.)

Error Limits

In all lessons, the error limit for the first reading is written on the board. The error limit for the story in lesson 6 is six. The rules are (1) if the students make seven or eight errors, the group is to reread the sentences that had mistakes and (2) if the students make nine or more errors, the group must reread the entire story before you present comprehension items. (See the rules at the end of Exercise 7, Sample Lesson 6, page 181.)

Reading Comprehension Activities

After the students read the entire story with the emphasis on accurately decoding words, they read the story with the emphasis on comprehension and relating the text to the pictures. The questions that you present to the students cover the full range of comprehension detail—from literal questions to prediction questions to questions that involve motives or require inferences about what happened in the story. (See Comprehension, Sample Lesson 6, pages 181–182.)

(See **Correcting Comprehension Errors During Selection Reading** on pages 48 and 49 of this guide for additional information regarding correcting comprehension errors.)

Independent Work

The scope-and-sequence chart on page 169 shows the main types of independent activities in lessons 1–35.

Some activities relate to the stories that students read during the lesson. Students write answers to written questions about the selection and sometimes complete sentences that correspond to story events. Some independent activities require students to follow written directions. In other activities, you will direct students to match (1) words with definitions or descriptions; (2) pictures with sentences or descriptions; and (3) story characters with quotes. Students follow rules for circling and crossing out displayed words or pictures, drawing missing pictures, and writing missing words. They also read short passages independently and write answers to questions about those selections.

Generally, the script has structured presentations to introduce each independent activity. Following a structured lesson, students are able to perform independently.

Students' independent work should be checked daily. The answer key shows what students are to do for each part of the worksheet.

Here are guidelines for checking the independent work.

1. Check as much as you can while students are doing their independent work.

2. Give students feedback on parts they did well on and any problems they are having. Oral feedback while students work is very effective: Nice job, Milton. You're really writing your letters carefully. Martha, one of those letters is backwards.

3. Require students to fix up any errors and show you the corrected paper.

4. Encourage students to take their worksheets home and share them with their parents. A possible plan is to send the worksheets home weekly, perhaps every Wednesday, accompanied by a sign-off sheet. A parent signs the sheet, and the student returns it to receive a bonus—possibly 3 points.

Independent work supplements everything the students are learning. The work gives students an opportunity to expand what they know and review both their knowledge and the skills they are learning.

(See Independent Work, Sample Lesson 6, page 182.)

Take-Home Stories

Take-home stories appear with each Mastery Test. These stories are similar to stories students have read in class. Each story needs to be removed from the workbook. Students fold each story into a four-page book that they color and later take home to read to family members.

These stories have the following objectives:

1. They provide students with a cumulative review of the words they have learned.

2. They permit the students to show off their reading skills to their families.

3. The stories are presented as a "book," which helps create a positive association between books and reading.

The sample take-home story below and its teacher's presentation accompany Mastery Test 1 (after lesson 7).

Take Home 1

EXERCISE 1

Rolla Slows Down

The next day when Rolla woke up, she looked in front of her and saw mountains and valleys. They were lovely. She couldn't see another horse anywhere in front of her. After a while, she found out that the other horses had made a painting and put it between her and horse 8. But Rolla didn't care. She felt wonderful leading all the horses into the mountains.

So everything is fine now. The horses are happy. The music sounds good. And the mothers and children like the merry-go-round even more than before.
The end.

One day, Rolla said to herself, "I am number 1, but I am right behind number 8." Rolla thought that she should be far away from number 8. Then it would look as if she was the leader and the other horses were following her.

a. Find Take-Home 1 on page 15 of your workbook. ✔

b. (Remove perforated story sheet. Direct students to fold sheet so the title is the cover page.)

c. This is like a story you read before. While I'm listening to each student read, you're going to make a storybook. You'll read each sentence in the story. When you're all finished, you'll color the picture and read your storybook to me. Be sure to read your story to someone at home.

d. (After testing all students, check out each student on reading the entire storybook.)

Step d of the exercise directs you to check out each student on reading the entire story. This step is very important. Tell students, It's a big privilege to take home a book like this. So let's make sure that you can read it well to your family and other people.

Making a Chart

At the end of the program, students make a chart that shows their favorite character in *Reading Mastery Signature Edition*, Transition Textbook. The chart serves as a basis for self-selected reading. Students select one of the stories that involves the most popular character. Here's the procedure for completing the chart.

1. Check that each student is looking at the worksheet chart. ✔

2. Call on individual students to read a few names on the chart until the entire chart is read.

3. Direct students to write the names of three of their favorite characters on the lines provided.

4. Conduct a vote for each character by reading each character's name.

Students raise their hand if they wrote that name. Students are then instructed to make **X**s on the chart to show how many students voted for that character. (Each **X** indicates one student who voted for that character. Note that there is space for 12 **X**s in each row.)

5. Students identify the character that is most popular (the one with the longest row of **X**s).

6. Students select stories about that character for the group to read.

Placement for Transition or Grade 2

(See Appendix A—Placement, pages 85–88.)

35

Name _____

POPULAR TEXTBOOK STORIES

Number of Students: _____

Who do students want to read about?		1	2	3	4	5	6	7	8	9	10	11	12
	The Bragging Rats												
	Tubby the Tug												
	Rolla												
	Molly and Bleep												
	Patty and the Cats												
	Goober												
	Honey and Sweetie												
	Dot and Dud												
	Boring Bill												

1. _____
2. _____
3. _____

Lesson 35   81

Mastery Tests

The Mastery Tests are scheduled after lessons 7, 16, 25 and 35. The Mastery Tests are designed to assess the performance of students on the most important decoding skills that were taught in the preceding lessons. Each test has a scoring system and criterion for remediating students or testing students for entering *Reading Mastery Signature Edition,* Grade 2. Mastery tests 1, 2 and 3 also have criterion for continuing in the *Reading Mastery Signature Edition,* Transition program.

The goal of these tests is not to evaluate the students' ability to learn, but rather to make sure that students are prepared for their next reading lessons in Transition or *Reading Mastery Signature Edition,* Grade 2.

- If students fail the test, they have not received the kind of instruction they need to pass the test. They must receive a remedy for their weak skills before they proceed in the program.

- If students meet the criterion for continuing in the program, but fail to meet the criterion to begin Grade 2, they need more instruction and practice in reading fluently. The following lessons in *Reading Mastery Signature Edition,* Transition provide instruction and practice of this type.

- If students meet the criterion, they can begin in Grade 2, or they can continue in Transition until they are ready to join a larger group beginning in Grade 2.

The tests consist of word reading and story reading. Each test is individually administered and takes about 2–3 minutes per student. It is usually possible to present the entire test and start on remedies during a single period.

The materials for the test (the words and selections that students read) appear on the worksheet page. Here's the student and teacher material for Mastery Test 1 (after lesson 7, before lesson 8).

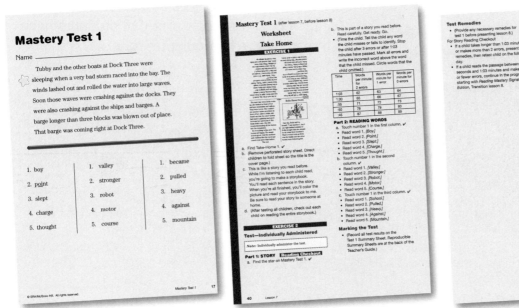

Administering the Tests

1. Identify a place for testing individual students that is beyond the hearing range of the other students in the group. This place should be quiet and have a minimum of distractions.

2. Present the various test items as specified in the teacher's presentation script. If the script does not indicate how students are to "read" a word, they can either read it the fast way or sound it out first.

3. Use the student's worksheet page to mark errors that the student makes in reading isolated words or story words. Errors include misidentifying the word and failing to respond to it.

The simplest procedure is to give the student your copy of the worksheet. Mark the errors on the student's copy. In this way, you will have a record of what the student did on all parts of the test.

If the student gets stuck, wait about 5 seconds, then tell the word and mark it as an error. The best way to record errors is to write what the student said for each sound or word that is misidentified.

- If the student calls the word **point,** "**paint,**" write **paint** above the word **point.**

- If the student reads a word that isn't in the story, write that word above where the student inserted it.

- If the student omits or fails to identify a word, circle the word.

4. After you test individual students, enter their data on the summary sheet for the test. There is one summary sheet for each of the four Mastery Tests. Each summary sheet lists items that students write or read on the test. (One sheet provides information for each group that takes the test.) Reproduce copies of the summary sheets and use them to record the students' progress. Note that the summary sheets also provide a database for awarding grades to students.

Specific Procedures for Administering Story Reading

Starting with Test 1, students individually read passages as part of the test. The student's performance is timed. Throughout the remainder of the program, tests measure the rate and accuracy of the students as they read passages.

Time limits for the Mastery Test stories are:
  Mastery Test 1, 1:03 minutes
  Mastery Test 2, 1:00 minute
  Mastery Test 3, 1:00 minute
  Mastery Test 4, 50 seconds

Mark the last word the student read within the allotted time. The stories are the same as or very similar to stories that students have read before in regular lessons.

Although there is a substantial difference in the rate of performance in readers, the passages are designed so that the student who is placed appropriately in the program should be able to read the story in under 1 minute and make no more than 2 errors. The directions for the story reading indicate that after a student makes 3 errors, you stop the student. Later, you'll administer remedies if a student goes over the time limit or makes more than 2 errors.

- If you arrange the individual testing so that you start with your higher performers, you can tell the others to look over the story and read it to themselves before they read it to you.

- Don't make the testing seem like a clinical situation that arouses anxiety. If you seem worried about the timing, the students will reflect your concern. They will try to read faster than they normally would and tend to make silly mistakes.

Remember the basic rule about reading rate: If students are going through the right steps to decode the word, they will tend to read faster and faster with practice. If they try to read faster without going through the right decoding steps, they will have problems.

If the student gets stuck on a word, wait about 5 seconds before telling the student the word. Don't let the student stew over it for a long time.

Make a mark after the last word read within the allotted time. Permit the student to continue reading until the passage has been completed or the error limit has been reached.

Scoring and Grading

Marking the Test

1. If students make mistakes on any of the items, mark the items.

2. For story reading, each word after the allotted time counts as an error.

3. Both parts are scored separately. A student could fail part 1 (Story Reading) and pass part 2 (Word Reading).

The summary sheet tells how many points each item is worth. Following is a summary sheet for Mastery Test 2 containing the results for a group of six students.

Part 1—Story Reading: Students who fail this part earn 30 points. For students who pass this part, deduct 5 points from the 55 points possible for each word that is read incorrectly, omitted, or inserted. The passing criterion is 2 errors or less (82%).

Part 2—Reading Words: Each word is worth 3 points. There are 45 points possible for part 2. The passing criterion is 3 errors or less (86%).

Textbook

EXERCISE 1

Reading Words

a. Open your textbook to lesson 6. Find the letter **L.** ✔
* (Teacher reference:)

1. <u>sound</u>ed	4. <u>valley</u>s
2. <u>follow</u>ing	5. <u>any</u>where
3. <u>mountain</u>s	6. <u>paint</u>ing

* You'll tell me the underlined part of each word and then tell me the whole word.
b. Word 1. What's the underlined part? (Signal.) *sound.*
* What's the whole word? (Signal.) *Sounded.*
c. Word 2. What's the underlined part? (Signal.) *follow.*
* What's the whole word? (Signal.) *Following.*
d. Word 3. What's the underlined part? (Signal.) *mountain.*
* What's the whole word? (Signal.) *Mountains.*
e. Word 4. What's the underlined part? (Signal.) *valley.*
* What's the whole word? (Signal.) *Valleys.*
f. Word 5. What's the underlined part? (Signal.) *any.*
* What's the whole word? (Signal.) *Anywhere.*
g. Word 6. What's the underlined part? (Signal.) *paint.*
* What's the whole word? (Signal.) *Painting.*
h. Let's read those words again the fast way.
* **Word 1. What word?** (Signal.) *Sounded.*
* (Repeat for remaining words: **following, mountains, valleys, anywhere, painting.**)

EXERCISE 2

Reading Words

a. Find the letter **A.** ✔
* (Teacher reference:)

1. phone	4. lovely
2. of course	5. robot
3. moving	

b. Word 1 is **phone.** What word? (Signal.) *Phone.*
Yes, answer the **phone.**
* **Phone** has a very strange spelling. Spell word 1. Get ready. (Tap 5 times.) *P-H-O-N-E.*
* What word? (Signal.) *Phone.*
c. The words for number 2 are **of course.** What words? (Signal.) *Of course.*
Of course, you know that.
* Spell **of.** Get ready. (Tap 2 times.) *O-F.*
* Spell **course.** Get ready. (Tap 6 times.) *C-O-U-R-S-E.*
* What words did you spell? (Signal.) *Of course.*
d. Spell word 3. Get ready. (Tap 6 times.) *M-O-V-I-N-G.*
* What word? (Signal.) *Moving.*
e. Spell word 4. Get ready. (Tap 6 times.) *L-O-V-E-L-Y.*
* What word? (Signal.) *Lovely.*
f. Spell word 5. Get ready. (Tap 5 times.) *R-O-B-O-T.*
* What word? (Signal.) *Robot.*
Yes, a **robot** is a machine that can do some of the things a human can do.
g. Let's read those words again the fast way.
* Word 1. What word? (Signal.) *Phone.*
* Number 2. What words? (Signal.) *Of course.*
* Word 3. What word? (Signal.) *Moving.*
* Word 4. What word? (Signal.) *Lovely.*
* Word 5. What word? (Signal.) *Robot.*

Reading Words

Words with O-I

a. Find the letter **M.** ✔
- (Teacher reference:)

1. p<u>oi</u>nt	3. b<u>oi</u>l
2. v<u>oi</u>ce	

b. You'll spell each word and then tell me the word.
c. Spell word 1. Get ready. (Tap 5 times.) *P-O-I-N-T.*
- What word? (Signal.) *Point.*
d. Spell word 2. Get ready. (Tap 5 times.) *V-O-I-C-E.*
- What word? (Signal.) *Voice.*
e. Spell word 3. Get ready. (Tap 4 times.) *B-O-I-L.*
- What word? (Signal.) *Boil.*
f. Let's read those words again the fast way.
- **Word 1. What word?** (Signal.) *Point.*
- (Repeat for remaining words: **voice, boil.**)

EXERCISE 4

Reading Words

a. Find the letter **R.** ✔
- (Teacher reference:)

1. spoke	4. together
2. wash	5. merry
3. awful	6. music

b. Word 1 is **spoke.** What word? (Signal.) *Spoke.*
   Yes, she **spoke** in a very low voice.
c. Word 2 is **wash.** What word? (Signal.) *Wash.*
   Yes, **wash** your hands and face.
d. Word 3 is **awful.** What word? (Signal.) *Awful.*
e. Word 4 is **together.** What word? (Signal.) *Together.*
f. Word 5 is **merry.** What word? (Signal.) *Merry.*
g. Word 6 is **music.** What word? (Signal.) *Music.*

h. Let's read those words again the fast way.
- **Word 1. What word?** (Signal.) *Spoke.*
- (Repeat for remaining words: **wash, awful, together, merry, music.**)

EXERCISE 5

Reading Words

Rhyming Words

a. Find the letter **S.** ✔
- (Teacher reference:)

1. sneak	4. gray
2. speak	5. nice
3. ray	6. mice

- These words are in rhyming pairs.
b. Spell word 1. Get ready. (Tap 5 times.) *S-N-E-A-K.*
- What word? (Signal.) *Sneak.*
c. Word 2 rhymes with **sneak.** What word? (Signal.) *Speak.*
d. Spell word 3. Get ready. (Tap 3 times.) *R-A-Y.*
- What word? (Signal.) *Ray.*
e. Word 4 rhymes with **ray.** What word? (Signal.) *Gray.*
   Yes, the sky was **gray.**
f. Spell word 5. Get ready. (Tap 4 times.) *N-I-C-E.*
- What word? (Signal.) *Nice.*
g. Word 6 rhymes with **nice.** What word? (Signal.) *Mice.*
h. Let's read those words again the fast way.
- **Word 1. What word?** (Signal.) *Sneak.*
- (Repeat for remaining words: **speak, ray, gray, nice, mice.**)

EXERCISE 6

Reading Words

a. Find the letter **P.** ✔
- (Teacher reference:)

1. sl<u>i</u>ces	3. perfect
2. people	4. toaster

- These are new words. You'll spell each word and then tell me the word.

b. Spell word 1. Get ready. (Tap 6 times.)
   S-L-I-C-E-S.
- What word? (Signal.) *Slices.*
  Yes, **slices** of bread.

c. Spell word 2. Get ready. (Tap 6 times.)
   P-E-O-P-L-E.
- What word? (Signal.) *People.*
  Yes, there were lots of **people** at the store.

d. Spell word 3. Get ready. (Tap 7 times.)
   P-E-R-F-E-C-T.
  Yes, she was a **perfect** reader.

e. Spell word 4. Get ready. (Tap 7 times.)
   T-O-A-S-T-E-R.
- What word? (Signal.) *Toaster.*
  Put bread in the **toaster.**

f. Let's read those words again the fast way.
- **Word 1. What word?** (Signal.) *Slices.*
- (Repeat for remaining words: **people, perfect, toaster.**)

Individual Turns

1. sounded
2. following
3. mountains
4. valleys
5. anywhere
6. painting

1. phone
2. of course
3. moving
4. lovely
5. robot

1. point
2. voice
3. boil

1. spoke
2. wash
3. awful
4. together
5. merry
6. music

1. sneak
2. speak
3. ray
4. gray
5. nice
6. mice

1. slices
2. people
3. perfect
4. toaster

- (Call on different children to read one or two of the words on the page.)

EXERCISE 7

Story Reading

a. (Write on the board:)

> **six**

- Everybody, tell me how many reading mistakes for this story. (Signal.) *Six.*

b. Find the story. ✔
- You'll read the title of the story. Get ready. (Tap for each word.) *Rolla . . . Slows . . . Down.*
- What happens in this story? (Call on a child. Idea: *Rolla slows down.*)

c. (Call on different children to read one or two sentences each.)

Rolla was very happy. She was horse number 1 on a merry-go-round. She went up and down with the music. The children were happy, and their mothers were happy.

Things went on like this for weeks. But then one day, something happened. Rolla said to herself, "I am number 1, but I am right behind number 8." Rolla thought that she should be far away from number 8. Then it would look as if she was the leader and the other horses were following her.

Rolla said, "I will get far from horse 8." To do that, Rolla slowed down. She went slower, and slower, and slower. But of course her plan didn't work. When she went slower, all the other horses went slower. The music slowed down and sounded awful. The mothers were unhappy. One of them said, "This merry-go-round is so slow you can't tell if it's going or if it has stopped."

d. Next page. ✔

The other horses were not happy with Rolla. Horse 2 kept shouting at Rolla, "Come on, Rolla. Let's get this merry-go-round moving." But Rolla tried as hard as she could to slow down.

At the end of the day, horse 8 was still there, right in front of her.

That evening, horse number 3 asked, "What are you trying to do?"

When Rolla told them, some of the horses started to laugh. Then horse number 5 said, "Rolla, would you be happy if you could not see horse 8?"

"Yes," Rolla said. "If I could not see that horse, I would not feel like I was following it. I would feel like the leader."

e. Next page. ✔

So the other horses got together and did a lot of talking. When they were done, they smiled and told Rolla they would fix things up.

The next day when Rolla woke up, she looked in front of her and saw mountains and valleys. They were lovely. She couldn't see another horse anywhere in front of her. After a while, she found out that the other horses had made a painting and put it between her and horse 8. But Rolla didn't care. She felt wonderful leading the other horses into the mountains.

So everything is fine now. The horses are happy. The music sounds good. And the mothers and children like the merry-go-round even more than before.

The end.

- (For no more than 6 errors, go to **Comprehension.**)
- (For 7 or 8 errors in the entire story, direct the rereading of the sentences in which mistakes occurred. Then go to **Comprehension.**)
- (For 9 or more errors, direct the rereading of the entire story. Then go to **Comprehension.**)

EXERCISE 8

Comprehension

- (Call on individuals to read one or two sentences each.)
- (Call on individuals to answer each question.)

a. Now you'll read the story again, and I'll ask questions.
b. Touch the title. ✔

ROLLA SLOWS DOWN

Rolla was very happy. She was horse number 1 on a merry-go-round. She went up and down with the music. The children were happy, and their mothers were happy.

- How did Rolla feel? [Idea: *Very happy.*]
- What made her feel happy? [Idea: *She was number 1.*]

Things went on like this for weeks. But then one day, something happened. Rolla said to herself, "I am number 1, but I am right behind number 8." Rolla thought that she should be far away from number 8. Then it would look as if she was the leader and the other horses were following her.

- What is bothering Rolla? [Idea: *She is right behind number 8.*]
- What horse is right in front of her? [Idea: *Number 8.*]
- Where does she want that horse to be? [Idea: *Far away.*]

Rolla said, "I will get far from horse 8." To do that, Rolla slowed down. She went slower, and slower, and slower. But of course her plan didn't work. When she went slower, all the other horses went slower. The music slowed down and sounded awful. The mothers were unhappy. One of them said, "This merry-go-round is so slow you can't tell if it's going or if it has stopped."

- What did Rolla do to try to get far from horse 8? [Idea: *Slowed down.*]
- Did her plan work? *[No.]*
- What did the other horses do? [Idea: *Went slower.*]
- What did the music do? [Idea: *Slowed down.*]
- How did that sound? [Idea: *Awful.*]

I can't tell if we are moving.

- Look at the picture. Rolla is slowing down. Is she getting far from horse 8? *[No.]*
- What's the mother saying? *[I can't tell if we are moving.]*
- That doesn't look like a lot of fun.

c. Next page. ✔

The other horses were not happy with Rolla. Horse 2 kept shouting at Rolla, "Come on, Rolla. Let's get this merry-go-round moving." But Rolla tried as hard as she could to slow down.

At the end of the day, horse 8 was still there, right in front of her.

That evening, horse number 3 asked, "What are you trying to do?"

When Rolla told them, some of the horses started to laugh. Then horse number 5 said, "Rolla, would you be happy if you could not see horse 8?"

"Yes," Rolla said. "If I could not see that horse, I would not feel like I was following it. I would feel like the leader."

- What did horse 5 ask Rolla? [Idea: *Rolla, would you be happy if you could not see horse 8?*]
- Would Rolla be happy if she could not see horse 8? *[Yes.]*

- Look at the picture. What is Rolla saying? *[I don't feel like the leader.]*
- She looks pretty sad. Do the other horses look sad? *[No.]*
- What are they thinking? *[Rolla is silly.]*
d. Next page. ✔

So the other horses got together and did a lot of talking. When they were done, they smiled and told Rolla they would fix things up.

The next day when Rolla woke up, she looked in front of her and saw mountains and valleys. They were lovely. She couldn't see another horse anywhere in front of her. After a while,

she found out that the other horses had made a painting and put it between her and horse 8. But Rolla didn't care. She felt wonderful leading the other horses into the mountains.

So everything is fine now. The horses are happy. The music sounds good. And the mothers and children like the merry-go-round even more than before.

The end.

- What did the other horses make for Rolla? [Idea: *A painting.*]
- Where did they put it? [Ideas: *Between her and horse 8; in front of her.*]

- Look at the picture. Everybody looks pretty happy. What is that mother saying? *[What a lovely merry-go-round.]*
- Look at Rolla. Can she see horse 8? *[No.]*
- What is Rolla thinking? *[I am the leader.]*

Lined Paper

Passage Reading
a. Find the passage. ✔
b. Later you'll read this passage and complete the items.

Workbook

Story Items
a. Open your workbook to lesson 6. Find the story items. ✔
b. Later you'll complete the items.

Character Matching Game

> *Note:* Instruct students who have not read Grade 1 stories to skip the blue words and blue pictures.

- • I am king of all the animals.

- • I am so strong I can move big ships.

- • I can't take the vow of a genie.

- • I want to find out more rules so I can get out of here.

- • I changed a frog into a king.

a. Find the character matching game. ✔
b. Later you'll draw lines to match the sentences with the pictures.

Writing Words for Pictures

a. Find the box of words. ✔
b. The first word in the box is **love.** Find the picture that shows love and write **love** under it.
   (Observe students and give feedback.)
c. Later you'll write the rest of the words under the pictures.

Independent Work Summary:

- Passage reading.
- Story items.
- Character matching game.
- Writing words for pictures.

END OF LESSON 6

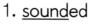

1. sounded
2. following
3. mountains
4. valleys
5. anywhere
6. painting

1. phone
2. of course
3. moving
4. lovely
5. robot

1. point
2. voice
3. boil

1. spoke
2. wash
3. awful
4. together
5. merry
6. music

1. sneak
2. speak
3. ray
4. gray
5. nice
6. mice

1. slices
2. people
3. perfect
4. toaster

Rolla Slows Down

Rolla was very happy. She was horse number 1 on a merry-go-round. She went up and down with the music. The children were happy, and their mothers were happy.

Things went on like this for weeks. But then one day, something happened. Rolla said to herself, "I am number 1, but I am right behind number 8." Rolla thought that she should be far away from number 8. Then it would look as if she was the leader and the other horses were following her.

Rolla said, "I will get far from horse 8." To do that, Rolla slowed down. She went slower, and slower, and slower. But of course her plan didn't work. When she went slower, all the other horses went slower. The music slowed down and sounded awful. The mothers were unhappy. One of them said, "This merry-go-round is so slow, you can't tell if it's going or if it has stopped."

The other horses were not happy with Rolla.
Horse 2 kept shouting at Rolla, "Come on, Rolla. Let's
get this merry-go-round moving." But Rolla tried as
hard as she could to slow down.

At the end of the day, horse 8 was still there, right
in front of her.

That evening, horse number 3 asked, "What are
you trying to do?"

When Rolla told them, some of the horses started
to laugh. Then horse number 5 said, "Rolla, would
you be happy if you could not see horse 8?"

"Yes," Rolla said. "If I could not see that
horse, I would not feel like I was following it. I would
feel like the leader."

So the other horses got together and did a lot of talking. When they were done, they smiled and told Rolla they would fix things up.

The next day when Rolla woke up, she looked in front of her and saw mountains and valleys. They were lovely. She couldn't see another horse anywhere in front of her. After a while, she found out that the other horses had made a painting and put it between her and horse 8. But Rolla didn't care. She felt wonderful leading the other horses into the mountains.

So everything is fine now. The horses are happy. The music sounds good. And the mothers and children like the merry-go-round even more than before.

The end.

A boy named Ted was always thinking. He would think in the morning. He would think when he ate lunch. He would think in school and at home. One day, his sister said to him, "Why do you spend so much time thinking?"

Ted said, "I don't know. Let me think about that."

So Ted thought about why he thought. This went on for five days.

Then he told his sister, "I don't know why I think so much. But I think I'm tired of thinking. Let's do something else."

So they went bike riding.

1. Who always thought?

2. He thought at home and in ▓▓▓▓.

3. Who asked him why he thought so much?

4. Did Ted know why he thought so much?

5. What did Ted and his sister do after Ted got tired of thinking?

Name _____

1. Rolla was unhappy because she was close to

   _____ .

   • a painting   • horse 8   • horse 2

2. What did Rolla do to get far from horse 8?

   _____

   • jumped up   • went faster   • went slower

3. When Rolla slowed down, what did the other horses do?

   _____

4. What did the music do? _____

5. Some of the other horses _____ .

   • went faster   • laughed at Rolla   • painted Rolla

6. When Rolla woke up the next morning, she saw

   _____ .

   • horse 8   • the moon and sun
   • mountains and valleys

7. Is Rolla happy now? _____

•

                                        • I am king of all the animals.

    •

                                        • I am so strong I can move
                                          big ships.

    •

                                        • I can't take the vow of a
                                          genie.

    •

                                        • I want to find out more
                                          rules so I can get out of
                                          here.

    •

                                        • I changed a frog into a
                                          king.

| love | angry | skates | light | school | picnic |

_____   _____   _____

_____   _____   _____